MEDIEVAL PHILOSOPHY

FROM 500 TO 1500 CE

The History of Philosophy

MEDIEVAL PHILOSOPHY

FROM 500 TO 1500 CE

EDITED BY BRIAN DUIGNAN, SENIOR EDITOR,
PHILOSOPHY AND RELIGION

Britannica®
Educational Publishing

IN ASSOCIATION WITH

ROSEN
EDUCATIONAL SERVICES

Published in 2011 by Britannica Educational Publishing
(a trademark of Encyclopædia Britannica, Inc.)
in association with Rosen Educational Services, LLC
29 East 21st Street, New York, NY 10010.

First Edition

Britannica Educational Publishing
Michael I. Levy: Executive Editor
J.E. Luebering: Senior Manager
Marilyn L. Barton: Senior Coordinator, Production Control
Steven Bosco: Director, Editorial Technologies
Lisa S. Braucher: Senior Producer and Data Editor
Yvette Charboneau: Senior Copy Editor
Kathy Nakamura: Manager, Media Acquisition
Brian Duignan: Senior Editor, Philosophy and Religion

Rosen Educational Services
Alexandra Hanson-Harding: Editor
Nelson Sá: Art Director
Cindy Reiman: Photography Manager
Matthew Cauli: Designer, Cover Design
Introduction by Brian Duignan

Library of Congress Cataloging-in-Publication Data

Medieval philosophy : from 500 to 1500 ce / edited by Brian Duignan. — 1st ed.
   p. cm. -- (The history of philosophy)
"In association with Britannica Educational Publishing, Rosen Educational Services."
Includes bibliographical references and index.
ISBN 978-1-61530-143-0 (library binding)
1. Philosophy, Medieval. I. Duignan, Brian.
B721.M459 2011
189—dc22

                                                        2010008836

Manufactured in the United States of America

On the cover: *Thomas Aquinas* Hulton Archive/Getty Images

On page 16: *Medieval manuscript showing a page from the works of Albertus Magnus* DEA/G.
Dagli Orti/De Agostini/Getty Images

Contents

INTRODUCTION

According to a view that was once conventional among historians, the European Middle Ages was an enormous setback to the intellectual progress of Western civilization. After the Western Roman Empire fell to invading barbarian armies in about 500 CE, most of the intellectual achievements of the Greco-Roman world–in philosophy, science, technology, art, literature, law, and government–were lost, forgotten, or destroyed, and Europe entered a millennium-long period (lasting to 1400–1500 CE) of intellectual and material decay. During much of this time, these scholars claimed, the vast majority of the European population lived in ignorance, superstition, poverty, and brutishness; virtually the only literate people on the continent were churchmen. Even the few universities, founded from the 11th century, reflected the continued stagnation of European society. The scholarship conducted in them was stale and unoriginal, consisting of dry commentaries on ancient texts and endless debate on insignificant problems—epitomized by the overdeveloped "angelology" (the study of the nature of angels) of the 13th century.

Philosophy throughout the Middle Ages, according to this view, was hampered, if not completely thwarted, by the imperative of conformity to the doctrines of the Roman Catholic Church. The role of philosophy was to justify or make rational sense of these doctrines using ancient concepts and methods as they were then understood. In later centuries the terms "Scholasticism" and "Scholastic," referring to the philosophy of the "schoolmen," were used in a justly pejorative sense to suggest

This 14th century painting shows, from left to right, Boethius, St. John Damascene, St. Dionysus the Areopagite (Pseudo-Dionysis), and St. Augustine. The figures behind them represent (left to right) Practical Theology, Hope, Faith, and Charity. Santa Maria Novella, Florence, Italy/The Bridgeman Art Library/Getty Images

pedantry, obsessive formalism, obscurity, and slavish adherence to intellectual authority.

Such was the common perception of medieval society and philosophy until about the mid-20th century. But it is now regarded as fundamentally mistaken. To be sure, many intellectual and artistic treasures of the ancient world were lost during the early Middle Ages (the period from 500 to about 1000 CE), but many also were preserved, notably through the painstaking efforts of monastic copyists. (Even much of what was lost did not actually disappear but was merely inaccessible, because almost no one could read Greek.) Although it is fair to say that the first few centuries of the Middle Ages were intellectually stagnant, the ensuing Carolingian period, named for the Frankish king and emperor Charlemagne (747–814 CE) and his immediate successors, was marked by a renewal of Latin education and scholarship, as well as by creative developments in architecture and the visual arts. During a second and much broader intellectual revival in the 11th and 12th centuries, the number monastic, ecclesiastical, cathedral, and private schools increased substantially.

Philosophy too was much richer than the conventional view assumed. Although most of its practitioners were theologians, and although most of them regarded philosophy as a tool for understanding—not challenging—the basic tenets of the Christian faith, in their hands ancient philosophy was developed and transformed in novel and sophisticated ways, and eventually it was applied to problems well beyond the realm of religion.

The medieval period in the history of Western philosophy is now recognized for its outstanding contributions to metaphysics, logic, and ethics, as well as to the philosophy of religion. In metaphysics, medieval philosophers explored the problem of universals (the question of whether there are independent entities corresponding to general terms such as "red" or "round") in unprecedented depth, developing theoretical alternatives that remain influential in contemporary discussions, and they produced intricate solutions to the problem of free will (the problem of reconciling human free will and divine foreknowledge of human actions). In logic, the medieval period is regarded as one of the three most productive and original in the history of the discipline—the other two being the ancient and Hellenistic periods and the late-19th to 20th centuries.

Even in the philosophy of religion the contributions of medieval philosophers were significant in their own right and not merely as justifications of Christian doctrine. For example, the so-called ontological argument for the existence of God (which infers God's existence from the idea of God itself) is still considered viable by some contemporary philosophers. Medieval discussions of the problem of evil (the problem of reconciling the existence of evil in the world with the supposed benevolence and omnipotence of God) also remain relevant for the fruitful lines of speculation they opened up.

By far the most important ancient philosophical influences on the development of philosophy in the Middle Ages were St. Augustine of Hippo (354–430 CE) and, much later, Aristotle (384–322 BCE). Until the rediscovery of Aristotle's works by Latin-speaking philosophers in the 12th and 13th centuries, medieval philosophy was conducted within the framework of Augustine's reconciliation of Christianity and Neoplatonism (the somewhat mystical philosophy of Plotinus [205–270 CE] and his followers, according to which all of reality is a series of emanations from a primal Unity, or One). The most influential features of Augustine's philosophy were: his distinction between the realm of the sensible and intelligible realms, the former being changeable and transitory, the latter unchangeable and eternal; his understanding of the soul as embodied in the sensible but connected to the intelligible; his analysis of knowledge as a kind of divine "illumination"; his conception of God as a primal Unity; and his solution to the problem of free will, which he based on the proposition that God has foreknowledge of the free acts of every human.

Augustine was perhaps most important for his conception of philosophy as an ally rather than an adversary of Christianity and as a means of understanding rather than refuting religious truths. This conception was influentially expressed by Boethius (c. 470 – 525 CE) in his counsel to philosophers of the future: "insofar as possible, join faith to reason."

Aristotle's philosophy was as important for the high Middle Ages (1000 – 1300 CE) as Augustine's was for the early Middle Ages. Starting in the 12th century, Neoplatonic notions of God, the soul, human nature, and the natural world gradually gave way to alternative understandings based on Aristotle's theories in physics, metaphysics, and ethics. In the late Middle Ages (1300 – 1500 CE), as various interpretations of Aristotelian philosophy developed into established schools with their own orthodoxies, some thinkers turned away from "The Philosopher" (as he was known) to embrace a form of mysticism inspired by the Neoplatonic philosophy of the early medieval period.

The first medieval philosopher of note, John Scotus Erigena (810 – c. 877 CE), a native of Ireland ("Erigena" means "Belonging to the People of Erin"), took part in the Carolingian renaissance as a member of the court of Charles II the Bald (823 – 877 CE). His De divisione naturae ("On the Division of Nature") was the first medieval attempt to explain the divine creation of the world in Neoplatonic terms. Unfortunately, church authorities decided that his work contained too much Neoplatonism and not enough Christianity, and it was condemned as heretical.

There followed a period of about 200 years during which little original philosophy was produced. In the 11th century, however, a few thinkers of lasting importance appeared, including St. Anselm and Peter Abelard (1079 – 1142 CE). Anselm, as already noted, invented the ontological argument. Abelard is remembered as the unfortunate lover of Heloise, the niece of a clergyman attached to the cathedral of Paris; at the instigation of her uncle, Abelard was castrated. His main contribution to philosophy was his solution to the problem of universals, which became the basis of the metaphysical school known as nominalism. (Nominalists deny that universals exist independently of particular things; realists assert that they do.)

The rise of the universities naturally resulted in the centralization of philosophical activity in university faculties. Both the form and content of philosophy were affected by this transformation; thereafter much philosophical writing consisted of commentaries on standard texts and formal analyses of disputed philosophical questions. The latter usually employed a pedagogical technique in which arguments on behalf of both the affirmative and the negative sides were thoroughly explored before a resolution was presented. This "dialectical" method is well illustrated in the Summa theologiae, by St. Thomas Aquinas (c. 1224-74) and in also in Abelard's Sic et Non ("Yes and No"). The inevitable formalism of such treatises became a focus of much misguided criticism in later centuries.

All of the major philosophers of the high Middle Ages were decisively influenced by Aristotle, despite the church's ultimately futile attempt to prohibit the teaching of Aristotelianism at the University of Paris in 1210. Aquinas, who was at that time the leading representative of medieval Aristotelianism adopted many aspects of Aristotle's metaphysics, including his conceptions of time, motion, and place; his fourfold analysis of causation; his notion of the "unmoved mover," which Aquinas identified with the God of Judaism and Christianity; and his fundamental distinctions between form and matter, substance and accident, and potentiality and actuality. Aquinas also relied on Aristotle's theory of the greatest good for human beings as activity in accord with virtue.

Of course, Aquinas did not simply disguise Aristotelian philosophy in theological dress; he rejected some Aristotelian doctrines (such as the eternity of the universe) and significantly modified others. Aspects of Aquinas's philosophy also reflect the influence of other ancient thinkers, especially St. Augustine. Although several of Aquinas's doctrines were condemned by the church shortly after his death, he was soon rehabilitated; he was canonized a saint in 1323 and named a doctor of the church in 1567. In the late 19th century Pope Leo XIII called for a revival of "Thomism," which thus became the semiofficial philosophy of the Roman Catholic Church until the Second Vatican Council (1962 – 65).

As a philosopher John Duns Scotus (c. 1266 – 1308 CE) was the equal of Aquinas in depth and subtlety, if not in lasting influence. (Scotus was known during his lifetime as Doctor Subtilis, or the "Subtle Doctor.") He made important contributions to logic, metaphysics, ethics, and the philosophy of religion. His extraordinarily complex proof of the existence of God (which incorporates the ontological argument) purports to show that there exists a being who is the first agent (effi-cient cause), the ultimate goal of movement or activity (final cause), and the preeminent, or maximally perfect, thing; such a being is also infinite and unique. Regarding the problem of universals, Scotus defended a complex form of realism, holding that, in addition to independently existing universals and the particular things in which they are instantiated, there is a special property of particular things, a "haeccity" or "thisness," that distinguishes each thing from all others.

The principle known as "Ockham's razor," formulated by the English philosopher William of Ockham (c. 1285– c. 1347 CE), is almost as well-known as the ontological argument and even more influential. In essence it recommends that one should not posit a plurality of entities or principles when a smaller number would suffice. By this means Ockham undertook to "trim" much unnecessary machinery from the elaborate metaphysical theories of some earlier medieval philosophers. The explanatory values of economy and simplicity encapsulated in Ockham's razor were soon extended beyond philosophy to the natural sciences, where their importance remains impossible to overstate. In science and philosophy—as indeed in any rational pursuit—a basic standard that any adequate theory must meet is that it account for all of the observed facts or phenomena in a simple and economical way.

Ockham's razor might suggest that its namesake was a nominalist (because a theory that asserts the reality of universals is necessarily more complex than one that denies them). Although Ockham was in fact a nominalist, he was not led to his nominalism by his razor; he simply believed that realist theories of universals were confused.

Any brief survey of medieval philosophy will inevitably neglect to mention many eminent thinkers, and this survey is no exception. Fortunately for the reader, this volume will discuss all the major medieval philosophers in depth and detail. Those who wish to understand the intellectual foundations of Christianity, to see how ancient philosophy continued to thrive long after the ancient world was dead, and to gain insight into profound human problems that transcend the boundaries of any religion are invited to enter.

serie p̃ces ebrietua.
ꝼessione requiet cordis
be resiste nescientes ad
gnũ ⁊ formidolosũ despa
te resilirunt· p̃cipu fi
tatis sponsatã xp̃o irri
ientes· p̃da libidis fluit illi
equicie crudelissimo nr̃o·

ue bissinũ dixim augustinũ
recte columpna fortissima ⁊ al
ma in domo dei cetis exposuer
supexcellit doctriaꝶ q̃ fluenta
habundant eructuãs uota ecc
irrigauit· fluctuantes hereti
cuꝶ crebꝰq̃ disputoibꝰ ꝗstuta

De plantamist

belue marine sunt testu
dines· que in gange fluuio ĩd
nascuntur· Rostrum hiis d
ni ⁊ caudam sedecim cubitoꝶ
longitudine hãt· Hiis solie
belue quas stacios uocant l
chus binus· Hiis uires sata
dicunt ut elephantos ad pͥ
uenientes morsibus infestent
eoꝶ promuscides abstraha

na animal De perna
armũ est· Er̃ animal
sum ac magnũ est ut d̃r
s· ⁊ nascitur ostrearꝰ mo
conchas· que conche coloꝛe
leum· Hoc monstrũ inͥ
herbas uestitur uelle nobi
fuluo nimis ac rutilo Vnͤ
nꝰ uestes p̃ciose ⁊ decorem
um uiroꝶ ac mulieꝶ ꝑe
n capitis fiut ex hiis que
in ornatum· ⁊ luxus fe
cm duplex· mirabiliͥ hr/tur
dei animalis· ⁊ cedit lux̃ͥ
exus De pisce igenti belua

Polipus piscis est De p
p̃ʒtus est ut dicit plin
qui reddit manibꝰq̃ brach
uitatur· Hic tenta uirtute
brachiis q̃ nautã de naui
ꝗcante stantem ut rapiat
hit ĩ mari· eiusq̃ carnibꝰ sa

gens belua est ut d̃r
ue stella p̃e oceanum ꝗ

CHAPTER 1

THE ROOTS OF MEDIEVAL PHILOSOPHY

*M*edieval philosophy designates the philosophical speculation that occurred in western Europe during the Middle Ages — i.e., from the fall of the western Roman Empire in the late 5th century CE to the Renaissance of the 15th century. During the European Middle Ages philosophy was closely connected to Christian thought, particularly theology, and the chief philosophers of the period were churchmen.

The roots of medieval philosophy lie in the thought of philosophers and theologians who lived during the last three centuries of the ancient period, especially Plotinus (205–270 CE) and the early Church Fathers — notably Origen (*c.* 185–*c.* 254), Victorinus (died *c.* 304), Gregory of Nyssa (*c.* 335–*c.* 394), Ambrose (339–397), Nemesius of Emesa (flourished 4th century), Augustine of Hippo (354–430), Pseudo-Dionysius the Areopagite (flourished *c.* 500), and Maximus the Confessor (*c.* 580–662). In the late 3rd and 4th centuries CE, Victorinus, Ambrose, and Augustine, among others, began to assimilate Neoplatonism — a mystical development of the thought of Plato (*c.* 428–*c.* 348 BCE) — into Christian doctrine in order to arrive at a rational interpretation of Christian faith. Thus, medieval philosophy was born of the confluence of Greek (and to a lesser extent of Roman) philosophy and Christianity. Plotinus, the founder of Neoplatonism, was already deeply religious, having come under the influence of Middle Eastern religions. Medieval philosophy continued to be characterized by this religious orientation. Its methods were at first those of Plotinus and, much later, those of Aristotle (384–322 BCE). But it developed within faith as a means of throwing light on the truths and mysteries of faith. Thus, religion and philosophy fruitfully cooperated in the Middle Ages. Philosophy, as the "handmaiden of theology," made possible a rational understanding of faith. Faith, for its part, inspired Christian thinkers to develop new philosophical ideas, some of which became part of the philosophical heritage of the West.

Toward the end of the Middle Ages, this beneficial interplay of faith and reason started to break down. Philosophy began to be cultivated for its own sake, apart from—and even in contradiction to—Christian religion. This divorce of reason from faith, made definitive in the 17th century by Francis Bacon (1561–1626) in England and René Descartes (1596–1650) in France, marked the birth of modern philosophy.

HISTORICAL BACKGROUND

The term *Middle Ages* refers to a period in European history that extended from the collapse of western Roman civilization in the 5th century CE to the Renaissance (variously interpreted as beginning in the 13th, 14th, or 15th century, depending on the region of Europe and on other factors). The term and its conventional meaning were introduced by Italian humanists engaged in a revival of classical learning and culture; their intent was self-serving, in that the notion of a thousand-year period of darkness and ignorance separating them from the ancient Greek and Roman world served to highlight the humanists' own work and ideals. In

This illustration shows Alaric before he invaded Rome. Bob Thomas/Popperfoto/Getty Images

a sense, the humanists invented the Middle Ages in order to distinguish themselves from it. The Middle Ages nonetheless provided the foundation for the transformations of the humanists' own Renaissance.

The sack of the city of Rome by Alaric the Visigoth in 410 CE had enormous impact on the political structure and social climate of the Western world, for the Roman Empire had provided the basis of social cohesion for most of Europe. Although the Germanic tribes that forcibly migrated into southern and western Europe in the 5th century were ultimately converted to Christianity, they retained many of their customs and ways of life; the changes in forms of social organization they introduced rendered centralized government and cultural unity impossible. Many of the improvements in the quality of life introduced during the Roman Empire—such as a relatively efficient agriculture, extensive road networks, water-supply systems, and shipping routes—decayed substantially, as did artistic and scholarly endeavours. This decline persisted throughout the so-called Dark Ages (also called Late Antiquity, or the Early Middle Ages), from the fall of Rome to about the year 1000, with a brief hiatus during the flowering of the Carolingian court during the rule of Charlemagne (747–814). Apart from that interlude, no large kingdom or other political structure arose in Europe to provide stability. The only force capable of providing a basis for social unity was the Roman Catholic Church. The Middle Ages, therefore, present the confusing and often contradictory picture of a society attempting to structure itself politically on a spiritual basis. This attempt came to a definitive end with the rise of artistic, commercial, and other activities anchored firmly in the secular world in the period just preceding the Renaissance.

After the dissolution of the western Roman Empire, the idea arose of Europe as one large church-state, called

Christendom. Christendom was thought to consist of two distinct groups of functionaries, the sacerdotium, or ecclesiastical hierarchy, and the imperium, or secular leaders. In theory, these two groups complemented each other, attending to people's spiritual and temporal needs, respectively. Supreme authority was wielded by the pope in the first of these areas and by the emperor in the second. In practice the two institutions were constantly sparring, disagreeing, or openly warring with each other. The emperors often tried to regulate church activities by claiming the right to appoint church officials and to intervene in doctrinal matters. The church, in turn, not only owned cities and armies but often attempted to regulate affairs of state.

Europe and the Mediterranean Lands about 1190 — from the Historical Atlas by William R. Shepherd, 1926. Courtesy of the University of Texas Libraries, The University of Texas at Austin

During the 12th century a cultural and economic revival took place; many historians trace the origins of the Renaissance to this time. The balance of economic power slowly began to shift from the region of the eastern Mediterranean to western Europe. The Gothic style developed in art and architecture. Towns began to flourish, travel and communication became faster, safer, and easier, and merchant classes began to develop. Agricultural developments were one reason for these developments; during the 12th century the cultivation of beans made a balanced diet available to all social classes for the first time in history. The population therefore rapidly expanded, a factor that eventually led to the breakup of the old feudal structures.

The 13th century was the apex of medieval civilization. The classic formulations of Gothic architecture and sculpture were achieved. Many different kinds of social units proliferated, including guilds, associations, civic councils, and monastic chapters, each eager to obtain some measure of autonomy. The crucial legal concept of representation developed, resulting in the political assembly whose members had *plena potestas*—full power—to make decisions binding upon the communities that had selected them. Intellectual life, dominated by the Roman Catholic Church, culminated in the 11th century in Scholasticism, a systematized and elaborately structured style of philosophy and philosophical instruction that dominated medieval universities until the early 15th century. Thomas Aquinas (c. 1224–74), the preeminent exponent of Scholasticism, achieved in his writings on Aristotle and the Church Fathers (the great Christian teachers and theologians of the 2nd to the 6th centuries CE) one of the greatest syntheses in Western intellectual history.

The breakup of feudal structures, the strengthening of city-states in Italy, and the emergence of national monarchies in Spain, France, and England, as well as such cultural developments as the rise of secular education, culminated in the birth of a self-consciously new age with a new spirit, one that looked all the way back to classical learning for its inspiration and that came to be known as the Renaissance.

ANCIENT PRECURSORS OF MEDIEVAL PHILOSOPHY

From the beginning of medieval philosophy, the natural aim of all philosophical endeavour to achieve the "whole of attainable truth" was clearly meant to include also the teachings of Christian faith. Although the idea of including faith had been expressed already by Augustine and the early Church Fathers, the principle was explicitly formulated by the pivotal, early 6th-century scholar Boethius (*c.* 470–524).

BOETHIUS

Born in Rome and educated in Athens, Boethius was one of the great mediators and translators, living in a narrow no-man's-land that divided late ancient philosophy from early medieval philosophy. His famous book, *De consolatione philosophiae (Consolation of Philosophy)*, was written while he, indicted for treachery and imprisoned by King Theodoric the Goth, awaited his own execution. It is true that the book is said to be, aside from the Bible, one of the most translated, most commented upon, and most printed books in world history; and that Boethius made (unfinished) plans to translate and to comment upon, as he said, "every book of Aristotle and all the dialogues of Plato." But his reputation as one of the founders of medieval

The consul Boethius holding sceptres in his left hand, ivory diptych, Byzantine, 5th–6th century; in the Museo Civico Cristiano, Brescia, Italy. SCALA/Art Resource, New York

philosophy refers to quite another side of his work. Strictly speaking, it refers to the last sentence of a very short tractate on the Holy Trinity, which reads, "As far as you are able, join faith to reason." Instead of "faith," such concepts as revelation, authority, or tradition could be (and, indeed, have been) cited; and "reason," though unambiguously meant to designate the natural powers of human cognition, could also be granted (and, in fact, has been granted) very different meanings. In any case, the connection between faith and reason postulated in this principle was from the beginning and by its very nature a highly explosive compound.

Boethius himself already carried out his program in a rather extraordinary way: although his *Opuscula sacra* ("Sacred Works") dealt almost exclusively with theological subjects, there was not a single biblical quotation in them: logic and analysis was all.

Boethius was destined to be for almost a millennium the last layperson in the field of European philosophy. His friend Cassiodorus (490–c. 585), author of the *Institutiones,* (an unoriginal catalog of definitions and subdivisions that nevertheless served as a sourcebook for the following centuries) occupied a position of high influence at the court of Theodoric (as did Boethius himself) and was also deeply concerned with the preservation of the intellectual heritage of the ancient world. Cassiodorus decided in his later years to quit his political career and to live with his enormous library in a monastery. This fact again is highly characteristic of the development of medieval philosophy: intellectual life needs not only teachers and students and not only a stock of knowledge to be handed down; there is also needed a certain guaranteed free area within human society, a kind of sheltered enclosure within which the concern for "nothing but truth" can exist and unfold. The Platonic Academy, as well as (for a limited time) the

This illustration on vellum from "De Consolatione Philosophiae cum Commento," shows Boethius in prison with students before his execution. Glasgow University Library, Scotland/The Bridgeman Art Library/ Getty Images

court of Theodoric, had been enclosures of this kind; but in the politically unsettled epoch to come "no plant would thrive except one that germinated and grew in the cloister."

PSEUDO-DIONYSIUS

The principle of the conjunction of faith and reason, which Boethius had proclaimed, and the way in which he himself carried it out were both based on a profound and explicit confidence in the natural intellectual capacity of human beings—a confidence that could possibly lead one day to the rationalistic conviction that there cannot be anything that exceeds the power of human reason to comprehend, not even the mysteries of divine revelation. To be sure, the great thinkers of medieval philosophy, in spite of their emphatic affirmation of faith and reason, consistently rejected any such rationalistic claim. But it must nonetheless be admitted that medieval philosophy on the whole, especially the systematic philosophies known as Scholasticism, contained within itself the danger of an overestimation of rationality, which recurrently emerged throughout its history.

On the other hand, there had been built in, from the beginning, a corrective and warning, which in fact kept the internal peril of rationalism within bounds—viz., the corrective exercised by the "negative theology" of the so-called Pseudo-Dionysius (flourished c. 500 CE), around whose writings revolved some of the strangest events in the history of Western culture. The true name of this protagonist is, in spite of intensive research, unknown. Probably it will remain forever an enigma why the author of several Greek writings (among them *On the Divine Names,* "On the Celestial Hierarchy," and *The Mystical Theology*) called himself "Dionysius the Presbyter" and, to say the least, suggested that he was actually Dionysius the Areopagite, a disciple of Paul the Apostle. In reality, almost all historians agree that Pseudo-Dionysius, as he came to be called, was probably a Syrian Neoplatonist, a contemporary of Boethius. Whatever the truth of the matter may be, his writings exerted an inestimable influence for more than 1,000 years by virtue of the somewhat surreptitious, quasi-canonical authority of their author, whose books were venerated, as has been said, "almost like the Bible itself." A 7th-century Greek theologian, Maximus the Confessor (c. 580–662), wrote the first commentaries on these writings; Maximus was followed over the centuries by a long succession of commentators, among them Albertus Magnus (c. 1200–80) and Aquinas. The main fact is that the unparalleled influence of Pseudo-Dionysius's writings preserved in the Latin West an idea, which otherwise could have been repressed and lost (since it cannot easily be coordinated with rationality)—that of a "negative" theology or philosophy that could act as a counterbalance against an excessive emphasis on the powers of human reason. It could be called an Eastern idea present and effective in the Occident. But after the break between the Eastern and Western churches in the Great Schism (1054), which erected a wall between East and West that lasted for centuries, Pseudo-Dionysius the Areopagite, having become himself (through translations and commentaries) a Westerner "by adoption," was the only one among all of the important Greco-Byzantine thinkers who penetrated into the schools of Western Christendom. Thus. negative theology was brought to medieval philosophy, as it were, through the back door.

The most important book of Pseudo-Dionysius, which dealt with the names that can be applied to God, exemplified his negative theology. It maintained first of all the decidedly biblical thesis that no appropriate name can be

Dionysius the Areopagite is shown converting the pagan philosophers in this painting. J. Paul Getty Museum. Los Angeles, USA/The Bridgeman Art Library/Getty Images

given to God at all unless he himself reveals it. But then Pseudo-Dionysius showed that even the revealed names, since they must be comprehensible to the finite understanding of humans, cannot possibly reach or express the nature of God; and that in consequence, every affirmative statement about God requires at once the corrective of the coordinate negation. The theologian cannot even call God "real" or "being," because he derives these concepts from the things to which God has given reality; and the Creator cannot possibly be of the same nature as that which he has created. Thus, *The Mystical Theology* concluded by finally relativizing also the negations, because God surpasses anything that humans may possibly say of him, whether it be affirmative or negative.

Medieval philosophers certainly could have learned all of this also from Augustine, who repeatedly warned that "Whatever you understand cannot be God." But probably an authority of even greater weight than Augustine was needed to counteract a reason that was tending to overrate its own powers; and this authority was attributed, although falsely, to the works of Dionysius the Areopagite. This impact could, of course, not be restricted to the idea of God; it necessarily concerned and changed the entire human conception of the world and of existence. The influence of Pseudo-Dionysius is reflected in the noteworthy fact that Aquinas, for instance, not only employed more than 1,700 quotations from Pseudo-Dionysius but also appealed almost regularly to his work whenever he spoke, as he often did (and in astonishingly strong terms), of the inexhaustible mystery of being. Aquinas, however, who also wrote a remarkable commentary on Pseudo-Dionysius's book *On the Divine Names,* is mentioned here only as an example, albeit a most telling example.

At the very end of the medieval era, Pseudo-Dionysius emerged once more in the work of a cardinal and mathematician, Nicholas of Cusa (1401–64), also known as an advocate of experimental knowledge, in whose library there are preserved several translations of the Areopagite writings—replete, moreover, with marginal notes in the cardinal's handwriting. But even without this concrete evidence, it would be quite plain that Nicholas's doctrine of "knowing nonknowing" is closely linked to Pseudo-Dionysius's conviction that all of reality is unfathomable.

The translation into Latin of the *Corpus Areopagiticum,* which was made in the 9th century—that is, some 400 years after the death of its author—by the Irish-born philosopher and theologian John Scotus Erigena (810–*c.* 877), is itself worthy of mention, especially because the translator was one of the most remarkable figures of early medieval philosophy. After generations of brave and efficient collectors, organizers, and schoolmasters had come and gone, Erigena, in his *De divisione natura* ("On the Division of Nature"), developed the Dionysian Neoplatonism on his own and tried to construct a systematic conception of the universe, a more or less pantheistic world view, which for a moment offered the Latin West the opportunity—or the temptation—to choose the way of the East once and for all. The church, though not until centuries later, condemned the book, apparently convinced that any counterbalance to its own position was dangerous in itself.

CHAPTER 2

THE EARLY MEDIEVAL PERIOD

The early medieval period, which extended to the 12th century, began with the collapse of ancient civilization in Western Europe and continued with the gradual building of a new, Christian culture in its place. Philosophy in these dark and troubled times was cultivated first by John Scotus Erigena and later by monks such as Anselm of Canterbury (c. 1033–1109). The monasteries became the main centres of learning and education and retained their preeminence until the founding of the cathedral schools and universities in the 11th and 12th centuries.

OVERVIEW OF EARLY MEDIEVAL PHILOSOPHY

Erigena, whose Latin name means "Belonging to the People of Erin [Ireland]," served as a master at the Carolingian court of Charles II the Bald (823–877). He translated into Latin some of the writings of the Church Fathers, and his own major work, *De divisione naturae* (862–866; *On the Division of Nature*), is a vast synthesis of Christian thought organized along Neoplatonic lines. For Erigena, God is the primal unity, unknowable and unnameable in himself, from which the multiplicity of creatures flows. He so far transcends his creatures that he is most appropriately called "superreal" and "supergood." Creation is the process of division whereby the many derive from the One. The One descends into the manifold of creation and reveals himself in it. By the reverse process, the multiplicity of creatures will return to their unitary source at the end of time, when everything will be absorbed in God.

If there was any philosophical-theological thinker of importance during the Middle Ages who remained untouched by the spirit of Pseudo-Dionysius, it was the 11th-century Benedictine monk Anselm of Canterbury, a highly cultivated Franco-Italian thinker, who is considered the first philosopher of Scholasticism. For years Anselm was prior and abbot of the abbey Le Bec in Normandy; he then became, somewhat violently, the archbishop of Canterbury. In Anselm's entire work there is not

St. Anselm (centre), *terra-cotta altarpiece by Luca della Robbia; in the Museo Diocesano, Empoli, Italy.* Alinari/Art Resource, New York

a single quotation from Pseudo-Dionysius; not even the name is mentioned. Consequently, Anselm's thinking, thus freed from the corrective embodied in Pseudo-Dionysius's negative theology, displayed a practically unlimited confidence in the power of human reason to illuminate even the mysteries of Christian faith; he thus frequently approached a kind of rationalism—the view that reason is the ultimate source or test of human knowledge. He did not shrink from the attempt to demonstrate, on compelling rational grounds, that salvation (for example) through God incarnate was philosophically necessary. To be sure, a theologian such as Anselm certainly would never have subscribed to the extreme thesis that nothing exists that is beyond the power of human reason to comprehend: the two famous phrases, coined by him and expressing again, in a grandiose formulation, the principle of Boethius, "faith seeking to be understood" and "I believe in order to understand," clearly proclaim his faith in the mysteries of revelation as comprising the very basis of all reasoning. Nevertheless, in the case of Anselm, the very peculiar conjunction of faith and reason was accomplished not so much through any clear intellectual coordination as through the religious energy and saintliness of an unusual personality. It was accomplished, so to speak, rather as an act of violence, which could not possibly last. The conjunction was bound to break up, with the emphasis falling either on some kind of rationalism or on a hazardous irrationalization of faith.

That this split did actually happen can be read to some extent in the fate of the "Anselmic argument," which the Enlightenment philosopher Immanuel Kant (1724–1804) was to reject as the "ontological proof of God"—though he connected it not with the name of Anselm but with that of René Descartes (1596–1650), the earliest modern philosopher. It is, in fact, significant that Descartes, in his proof of the existence of God, imagined that he was saying the same thing as Anselm, and that, on the other hand, Anselm would scarcely have recognized his own argument had he encountered it in the context of Descartes's *Discours de la méthode* (1637; *Discourse on Method*), which claims to be "pure" philosophy based upon an explicit severance from the concept of God held by faith. But given Anselm's merely theoretical starting point, that severance was not only to be expected; it was almost inevitable.

But, also within the framework of medieval Scholasticism, a dispute was always brewing between the dialecticians, who emphasized or overemphasized reason, and those who stressed the suprarational purity of faith. Berengar of Tours (*c.* 999–1088), an 11th-century logician, metaphysician, and theologian, who was fond of surprising formulations, maintained the preeminence of thinking over any authority, holding in particular that the real presence of Christ in the Eucharist was logically impossible. His contemporary the Italian hermit-monk and cardinal Peter Damian (1007–72), however—who was apparently the first to use the ill-famed characterization of philosophy as the "handmaiden of theology"—replied that if God's omnipotence acts against the principle of contradiction, then so much the worse for the science of logic. Quite analogous to the foregoing controversy, though on a much higher intellectual level, was the bitter dispute that took place almost one century later between a Cistercian reformer, Bernard of Clairvaux (1090–1153), and a logician and theologian, Peter Abelard (1079–1142). Bernard, a vigorous and ambivalent personality, was in the first place a man of religious practice and mystical contemplation, who, at the end of his dramatic life, characterized his odyssey as that of *anima quaerens Verbum,* "a soul in search of the Word." Although he by no means rejected philosophy on principle, he looked with deep suspicion upon the primarily logical approach to theology espoused by Abelard. "This man," said Bernard, "presumes to be able to comprehend by human reason the entirety of God."

Logic was at that time, as a matter of fact, the main battleground of all Scholastic disputations. "Of all philosophy, logic most appealed to me," said Abelard, who by "logic" understood primarily a discipline not unlike certain present-day approaches, the "critical analysis of thought on the basis of linguistic expression." From this viewpoint (of linguistic logic), Abelard also discussed with penetrating sharpness the nature of universals. (A universal is a quality or property that each individual member of a class of things must possess if the same general word is to apply to all the things in that class. Redness, for example, is a universal possessed by all red objects.) The "problem of universals" is the question of whether universals are concepts, verbal expressions, or a special kind of entity that exists independently, outside space and time. As is well known, it has been asserted that the problem of universals was the principal, or even the only, subject of concern in medieval Scholasticism—a charge that is misleading, although the problem did greatly occupy philosophers from the time of Boethius. Their main concern from the beginning was the whole of reality and existence.

The advance of medieval thought to a highly creative level was foreshadowed, in those very same years before Peter Abelard died, by Hugh of Saint-Victor (1096–1141), an Augustinian monk of German descent, when he wrote *De sacramentis Christianae fidei* ("On the Sacraments of the Christian Faith"), the first book in the Middle Ages that could rightly be called a *summa,* or comprehensive treatise; in its introduction, in fact, the term itself is used as meaning a comprehensive view of all that exists (*brevis quaedam summa omnium*). To be sure, its author stands wholly in the tradition of Augustine and Pseudo-Dionysius; yet he is also the first medieval theologian to proclaim an explicit openness toward the natural world. Knowledge of reality is, in his understanding, the prerequisite for contemplation; each of the seven liberal arts aims "to restore God's image in us." "Learn everything," he urged; "later you will see that nothing is superfluous."

It was on this basic that the university—which was not the least of the achievements of medieval Scholasticism— was to take shape. And it was the University of Paris, in particular, that for some centuries was to be the most representative university of the West. Although there are usually a variety of reasons and causes for such a development, in this case the importance of the university—unlike that of Bologna and also of Oxford—lay mainly in the fact that it was founded in the most radical way upon those branches of knowledge that are "universal" by their very nature: upon theology and philosophy. It is, thus, remarkable, though not altogether surprising, that there seems to have existed not a single *summa* of the Middle Ages that did not, in some way or other, derive from the University of Paris.

Strangely enough, the classical theological-philosophical textbook used in the following centuries at the universities of the West was not the first *summa,* composed by Hugh of Saint-Victor, but was instead a work by Peter Lombard (*c.* 1100–60), a theologian who probably attended Abelard's lectures and who became *magister* at the cathedral school of Notre-Dame and, two decades later, bishop of Paris. Lombard's famous *Four Books of Sentences,* which, though written one or two decades later than Hugh's *summa,* belonged to an earlier historical species, contained about 1,000 texts from the works of Augustine, which comprise nearly four-fifths of the whole. Much more important than the book itself, however, were the nearly 250 commentaries on it, by which—into the 16th century—every master of theology had to begin his career as a teacher. In view of this wide usage, it is not astonishing that Lombard's book underwent some transformations, at the hands, for instance, of its most ingenious commentator, Aquinas, but also (and even more so) at the hands of John Duns Scotus (c. 1266–1308) in his *Opus Oxoniense,* which, in spite of being a work of extremely personal cast, was outwardly framed as a commentary on the "Master of Sentences."

The remainder of this chapter will discuss in detail the lives and work of the most important philosophers and theologians of the early medieval period.

JOHN SCOTUS ERIGENA

(b. 810, Ireland—d. c. 877)

John Scotus Erigena was a philosopher and theologian and a translator and commentator on several earlier authors in works integrating Greek and Neoplatonist philosophy with Christian belief.

From about 845, Erigena lived at the court of the West Frankish king Charles II the Bald, near Laon (now in France), first as a teacher of grammar and dialectics (logical argumentation). He participated in theological disputes over the Eucharist and predestination and set forth his position on the latter in *De predestinatione* (851; "On Predestination"), a work condemned by church authorities. Erigena's translations of the Greek Church Fathers Pseudo-Dionysius, Maximus the Confessor, Gregory of Nyssa, and Epiphanius, commissioned by Charles, made those writings accessible to Western thinkers.

Erigena's familiarity with dialectics and with the ideas of his theological predecessors was reflected in his principal work, *De divisione naturae* (862–866; "On the Division of Nature"), an attempt to reconcile the Neoplatonist doctrine of emanation with the Christian tenet of creation. The work classifies nature into (1) that which creates and is not created; (2) that which creates and is created; (3) that which does not create and is created; and (4) that which does not create and is not created. The first and the fourth are God as beginning and end; the second and third are the dual mode of existence of created beings (the intelligible and the sensible). The return of all creatures to God begins with release from sin, physical death, and entry into the life hereafter. The human individual, for Erigena, is a microcosm of the universe because he has senses to perceive the world, reason to examine the intelligible natures and causes of things, and intellect to contemplate God. Through sin, humans' animal nature has predominated, but through redemption they become reunited with God.

Although highly influential upon Erigena's successors, notably the Western mystics and the 13th-century Scholastics, *De divisione naturae* eventually suffered condemnation by the church because of its pantheistic implications.

BERENGAR OF TOURS

(b. *c.* 999, probably Tours, Touraine [now in France]—d. Jan. 10, 1088, priory of Saint-Cosme, near Tours)

Berengar of Tours was a theologian who was the leader of the losing side in the crucial eucharistic controversy of the 11th century.

Having studied under the celebrated Fulbert at Chartres, Berengar returned to Tours after 1029 and became canon of its cathedral and head of the School of Saint-Martin, which rivaled Bec under Lanfranc, who was later to be his opponent. Berengar befriended Geoffrey, Count of Anjou, and Eusebius Bruno, later bishop of Angers. About 1040 he was appointed archdeacon of Angers.

Shortly thereafter, Berengar, who always exhibited great independence of thought, began to teach ideas contrary to prevailing beliefs. Most notably, he rejected the then-current view of transubstantiation credited to the 9th-century abbot of Corbie, Paschasius Radbertus, who professed that the bread and wine, after consecration in the mass, became the real body and blood of Christ. Berengar favoured the interpretation formulated in *De corpore et sanguine Domini* ("Concerning the Body and Blood of the Lord") by Ratramnus, a monk of Corbie, to whom the elements became the body and blood of Christ in a symbolic sense. Berengar's restatement of these views aroused severe opposition. He boldly wrote (*c.* 1050) to Lanfranc against his condemning Ratramnus. The letter arrived in Lanfranc's absence and, after being read by several persons, finally reached him at Rome. Pope Leo IX excommunicated Berengar at the Easter Synod of 1050 and ordered him to the Council of Vercelli (1050). Berengar reluctantly obeyed. He went to Paris to get permission from the French king Henry I, his nominal abbot, to attend the synod. He was imprisoned by Henry and condemned at Vercelli in absentia.

On his release from prison, Berengar took refuge with his protector, Geoffrey, and Henry ordered a synod at Paris to judge Berengar and his supporter Eusebius. The synod condemned them both (1051). In 1054 the powerful papal legate Cardinal Hildebrand came to France to preside at the Synod of Tours. To preserve peace, a compromise was reached under which Berengar signed a vague eucharistic statement. In 1059 he was summoned to Rome for another council, at which he was refused a hearing and was asked to sign an extreme statement repugnant to his ideas. After this, Geoffrey died, and Eusebius began to draw away from Berengar. Berengar nevertheless published a treatise (c. 1069) against the Roman council of 1059, which was answered by Hugo of Langres and by Lanfranc, with a rejoinder by Berengar.

Berengar's position was steadily worsening, and the rigorous pattern of examination, condemnation, and recantation was repeated at the nearly violent Council of Poitiers (1076), the Roman synods of 1078 and 1079, and a trial at Bordeaux in 1080. Thereafter Berengar was silent. He retired to ascetic solitude in the priory of Saint-Cosme.

Berengar's eucharistic doctrine is expressed in his *De sacra coena* ("On the Holy Supper"), written in reply to Lanfranc. More than any of his contemporaries, Berengar applied to theological development the method of dialectic. He based his argument on the belief that Paschasius's view was contrary to the Scriptures, the Church Fathers, and reason.

SAINT PETER DAMIAN

(b. 1007, Ravenna [Italy]—d. Feb. 22, 1072, Faenza)

Peter Damian was a cardinal and doctor of the church, an original leader and a forceful figure in the Gregorian Reform movement, whose personal example and many writings exercised great influence on religious life in the 11th and 12th centuries.

EARLY LIFE AND CAREER

Little is known for certain about Peter Damian's early life before his entrance into the hermitage of Fonte Avellana in the diocese of Gubbio (now Cagli-Pergola, Italy) in the Apennines. The facts must be pieced out primarily from his surviving letters and from his biography by John of Lodi. These documents reveal that Damian's parents died shortly after his birth and that an older brother raised him and gave him his initial education in Ravenna. Beginning in his early teens, Damian spent at least 10 years studying the liberal arts at Ravenna, Faenza, and Parma. His writings throughout his life indicate a broad knowledge of Classical and Christian works, training that helped make Damian one of the finest Latin stylists of the Middle Ages. Eventually he taught rhetoric at Ravenna, remaining in that position for about five years before becoming a hermit.

While teaching in Ravenna, Damian seems to have been influenced by the ideas of St. Romuald, who was instrumental in promoting the eremitical (hermetic) ideal in Italy in the late 10th and the early 11th century. Not only did Damian write Romuald's biography, but about 1035, having possibly already become a cleric, he entered the hermitage of Fonte Avellana, which had been established by Romuald's disciples. By the mid-1040s Damian had become the prior of this house, which combined the essential elements of Benedictine monasticism with the higher calling of eremitical asceticism. At Fonte Avellana he emphasized the ideal of apostolic poverty, which later became so important in Western spirituality. Going forth, he founded a number of monasteries and reformed others according to the practices established at Fonte Avellana.

His reform efforts drew the attention of both the pope and the German emperor Henry III. As a result, Damian was actively involved in the imperial efforts to transform the papacy in the late 1040s and worked with Pope Leo IX (reigned 1049–54) to spread that reform throughout the church in the West. The ideals of the reform movement are particularly evident in Damian's tract *Liber gratissimus* (1052; "Most-Favoured Book"), which treated the problem of simony (the purchase of ecclesiastical office) and the validity of the sacraments bestowed by a simoniac cleric. Although he strongly condemned the purchase of office by clergymen, Damian defended the validity of the sacraments they administered. In *Liber Gomorrhianus* ("Book of Gomorrah"), written about 1051, he addressed the other central concern of reformers during this period, the question of celibacy versus clerical marriage (nicolaitism). His rhetorical advocacy of celibacy was so excessive, however, that Pope Leo chose not to give it the unconditional support he offered to Damian's tract on simony. Despite this setback, Damian's efforts in support of the reforming papacy were rewarded by Pope Stephen IX, who appointed him the cardinal-bishop of Ostia in 1057. Damian immediately became one of the most important members of the college of cardinals and played a significant part in preparing the decree on papal elections of April 1059 in which the cardinals declared their right to select the pope and the manner in which the selection would be made.

Damian's extraordinary knowledge of canon law, in particular of the *Decretum* of Burchard of Worms, and his dedicated service to the papacy and the universal church made him an excellent choice to serve in papal embassies. In 1059–60, for example, he undertook a mission to the troubled archdiocese of Milan to arbitrate the struggle between the archbishop and the Patarines, who were over-zealous in their attacks on clerical concubinage. In 1063 he traveled to the monastery of Cluny (now in France) to serve as arbiter in the dispute between Abbot Hugh (St. Hugh of Cluny) and Bishop Drogo of Mâcon in the matter of Cluniac exemptions from episcopal control. Damian also represented the papacy in 1069 in an effort to dissuade Henry IV of Germany from divorcing his wife, Bertha. His final mission, so appropriate as his last act of service for the papacy, was in 1072 to Ravenna, the place of his birth, where he tried to restore harmony between that see and Rome. On his return later that year, he died in the monastery of Faenza. His missions to Germany and Ravenna, however, were exceptions to the routine of his later years, for he had established himself in semiretirement at Fonte Avellana after 1067.

ASSESSMENT

In addition to many letters and theological tracts, his abundant and varied writings include 53 sermons, 7 vitae (saints' lives), and liturgical pieces. Two tracts in particular merit special note. The first, a tract against the Jews, must be viewed in the light of the growing anti-Semitism of the 11th century; the other, his most important theological tract, De divina omnipotentia ("On Divine Omnipotence"), reveals both the profundity of his thought and the extraordinary eloquence of his pen.

His legacy is also evident in his work in the service of the papacy. As a member of the College of Cardinals, he not only served frequently as a papal ambassador but also was a confidant of Popes Stephen IX, Nicholas II, and Alexander II. His positions on the issues of simony and nicolaitism were very important in shaping the papal stances on these matters. From 1055 to 1072, Damian, Cardinal Humbert of Silva Candida, and Cardinal Hildebrand (the future Pope Gregory VII) formed a powerful trio in the College of Cardinals who helped to lay the foundations for the medieval papacy and give structure to the church of the central Middle Ages and beyond.

Moreover, Damian's championship of the eremitical ideal helped to establish firmly the link between Byzantine eremitism and the Western Benedictine ideal. In so doing, he prepared the way for the individual spirituality seen in the *vita apostolica* ("apostolic life"), the supreme example of which is St. Francis of Assisi. Damian was declared a doctor of the church in 1828.

SAINT ANSELM OF CANTERBURY

(b. 1033/34, Aosta, Lombardy—d. April 21, 1109, possibly at Canterbury, Kent, Eng.)

Anselm was the founder of Scholasticism and the originator of what came to be known as the ontological argument for the existence of God, which is based on the notion that the idea of an absolutely perfect being is itself a demonstration of such a being's existence. He is also credited with the satisfaction theory of atonement or redemption, according to which atonement is a matter of making satisfaction or recompense to God for offenses committed by human beings. Incomplete evidence suggests that he was canonized in 1163.

EARLY LIFE AND CAREER

Anselm was born in the Piedmont region of northwestern Italy. His birthplace, Aosta, was a town of strategic importance in Roman imperial and in medieval times, because it stood at the juncture of the Great and Little St. Bernard routes. His mother, Ermenberga, belonged to a noble Burgundian family and possessed considerable property. His father, Gondolfo, was a Lombard nobleman who intended that Anselm would make a career of politics and did not approve of his early decision to enter the monastic life.

Canterbury Cathedral. Peter Macdiarmid/Getty Images

Anselm received an excellent classical education and was considered one of the better Latinists of his day. His early education impressed on him the need to be precise in his use of words, and his writings became known for their clarity.

In 1057 Anselm left Aosta to enter the Benedictine monastery at Bec (located between Rouen and Lisieux in Normandy, France), because he wanted to study under the monastery's renowned prior, Lanfranc. While on his way to Bec, he learned that Lanfranc was in Rome, so he spent some time at Lyon, Cluny, and Avranches before entering the monastery in 1060. In 1060 or 1061 he took his monastic vows. Because of Anselm's reputation for great intellectual ability and sincere piety, he was elected prior of the monastery after Lanfranc became abbot of Caen in 1063. In 1078 he became abbot of Bec.

In the previous year (1077), Anselm had written the *Monologium* ("Monologue") at the request of some of his fellow monks. A theological treatise, the *Monologium* was both apologetic and religious in intent. It attempted to demonstrate the existence and attributes of God by an appeal to reason alone rather than by the customary appeal to authorities favoured by earlier medieval thinkers. Moving from an analysis of the inequalities of various aspects of perfection, such as justice, wisdom, and power, Anselm argued for an absolute norm that is everywhere at all times, above both time and space, a norm that can be comprehended by the human mind. Anselm asserted that the norm is God, the absolute, ultimate, and integrating standard of perfection.

THE ONTOLOGICAL ARGUMENT

Under Anselm, Bec became a centre of monastic learning and some theological questioning. Lanfranc had been a renowned theologian, but Anselm surpassed him. He continued his efforts to answer satisfactorily questions concerning the nature and existence of God. His *Proslogium* ("Address," or "Allocution"), originally titled *Fides quaerens intellectum* ("Faith Seeking Understanding"), established the ontological argument for the existence of God. In it he argued that even a fool has an idea of a being greater than which no other being can be conceived to exist; that such a being must really exist, for the very idea of such a being implies its existence. Anselm's later work, the *Proslogium* (1077/78; "Allocution" or "Address"), contains his most famous proof of the existence of God. This begins with a datum of faith: Humans believe God to be the being than which none greater can be conceived. Some, like the fool in the Psalms, say there is no God; but even the fool, on hearing these words, understands them, and what he understands exists in his intellect, even though he does not grant that such a being exists in reality. But it is greater to exist in reality and in the understanding than to exist in the understanding alone. Therefore, it is contradictory to hold that God exists only in the intellect, for then the being than which none greater can be conceived is one than which a greater can be conceived—namely, one that exists both in reality and in the understanding.

Anselm's ontological argument was challenged by a contemporary monk, Gaunilo of Marmoutier, in the *Liber pro insipiente,* or "Book in Behalf of the Fool Who Says in His Heart There Is No God." Gaunilo denied that an idea of a being includes existence in the objective order and that a direct intuition of God necessarily includes God's existence. Anselm's wrote in reply, his *Liber apologeticus contra Gaunilonem* ("Book [of] Defense Against Gaunilo"), which was essentially a repetition of the ontological argument of the *Proslogium.*

APPOINTMENT AS ARCHBISHOP OF CANTERBURY

William the Conqueror, who had established Norman overlordship of England in 1066, was a benefactor of the monastery at Bec, to which he granted lands in both England and Normandy. Anselm made three visits to England to view these lands. During one of those visits, while Anselm was founding a priory at Chester, William II Rufus, the son and successor of William the Conqueror, named him archbishop of Canterbury (March 1093). The see had been kept vacant since the death of Lanfranc in 1089, during which period the king had confiscated its revenues and pillaged its lands.

Anselm accepted the position somewhat reluctantly but with an intention of reforming the English church. He refused to be consecrated as archbishop until William restored the lands to Canterbury and acknowledged Urban II as the rightful pope against the antipope Clement III. In fear of death from an illness, William agreed to the conditions, and Anselm was consecrated on Dec. 4, 1093. When William recovered, however, he demanded from the new archbishop a sum of money, which Anselm refused to pay lest it look like simony. In response to Anselm's refusal, William refused to allow Anselm to go to Rome to receive the pallium—a mantle, the symbol of papal approval of his archiepiscopal appointment—from Urban II, lest this be taken as an implied royal recognition of Urban. In claiming that the king had no right to interfere in what was essentially an ecclesiastical matter, Anselm became a major figure in the investiture controversy, concerning the question as to whether a secular ruler (e.g., emperor or king) or the pope had the primary right to invest an ecclesiastical authority, such as a bishop, with the symbols of his office.

The controversy continued for two years. On March 11, 1095, the English bishops, at the Synod of Rockingham, sided with the king against Anselm. When the papal legate brought the pallium from Rome, Anselm refused to accept it from William, since it would then appear that he owed his spiritual and ecclesiastical authority to the king. William permitted Anselm to leave for Rome, but on his departure he seized the lands of Canterbury.

Anselm attended the Council of Bari (Italy) in 1098 and presented his grievances against the king to Urban II. He took an active part in the sessions, defending the doctrine of the *Filioque* ("and from the Son") clause in the Nicene-Constantinopolitan Creed against the Greek Church, which had been in schism with the Western Church since 1054. The *Filioque* clause, added to the Western version of the Creed, indicated that the Holy Spirit proceeded from the Father and Son. The Greek

Church rejected the *Filioque* clause as a later addition. The Council also reapproved earlier decrees against the investiture of ecclesiastics by lay officials.

THE SATISFACTION THEORY OF REDEMPTION

When Anselm left England, he had taken with him an incomplete manuscript of his work *Cur Deus homo?* ("Why Did God Become Man?"). After the Council of Bari, he withdrew to the village of Liberi, near Capua, and completed the manuscript in 1099. This work became the classic treatment of the satisfaction theory of redemption. According to this theory, which is based upon the feudal structure of society, finite humanity has committed a crime (sin) against infinite God. In feudal society, an offender was required to make recompense, or satisfaction, to the one offended according to that person's status. Thus, a crime against a king would require more satisfaction than a crime against a baron or a serf. According to this way of thinking, finite humans, since they could never make satisfaction to the infinite God, could expect only eternal death. The instrument for bringing humans back into a right relationship with God, therefore, had to be the God-human (Christ), by whose infinite merits humans are is purified in an act of cooperative re-creation. Anselm rejected the view that humans, through their his sin, owes a debt to the devil, and placed the essence of redemption in individual union with Christ in the Eucharist (Lord's Supper), to which the sacrament of Baptism (by which a person is incorporated into the church) opens the way.

After completing *Cur Deus homo?* Anselm attended a council at the Lateran (papal palace) in Rome at Easter 1099. One year later, William Rufus died in a hunting accident under suspicious circumstances, and his brother Henry I seized the English throne. In order to gain ecclesiastical support, he sought for and secured the backing of Anselm, who returned to England. Anselm soon broke with the King, however, when Henry insisted on his right to invest ecclesiastics with the spiritual symbols of their office. Three times the King sought an exemption, and each time the Pope refused. During this controversy, Anselm was in exile, from April 1103 to August 1106. At the Synod of Westminster (1107), the dispute was settled. The King renounced investiture of bishops and abbots with the ring and crosier (staff), the symbols of their office. He demanded, however, that they do homage to him prior to consecration. The Westminster Agreement was a model for the Concordat of Worms (1122), which settled for a time the lay-investiture controversy in the Holy Roman Empire.

Anselm spent the last two years of his life in peace. In 1163, with new canons requiring approvals for canonization (official recognition of persons as saints), Archbishop Thomas Becket of Canterbury (1118?–1170) referred Anselm's cause to Rome. Anselm was probably canonized at this time, for the Canterbury records for 1170 make frequent mention of the pilgrimages to his new shrine in the cathedral. For several centuries he was venerated locally. Clement XI (pope from 1700 to 1721) declared Anselm a doctor (teacher) of the church in 1720.

ROSCELIN

(b. c. 1050, Compiègne, France—d. c. 1125)

Roscelin was a French philosopher and theologian known as the originator of an extreme form of nominalism, holding that universals are nothing more than verbal expressions. (As mentioned earlier, a universal is a quality or property that each individual member of a class of things must possess if the same general word is to apply to all the things in that class.) His only extant work seems to be a letter to Peter Abelard, who studied under him at Besançon; the little that is otherwise known of Roscelin's doctrines is derived from the works of Anselm and of Abelard and from the anonymous work *De generibus et speciebus* ("Of Generals and Specifics"). Roscelin retracted his doctrine on the Trinity—namely, that it consisted of three separate persons in God—when it was declared heretical by the Council of Soissons in 1092.

WILLIAM OF CHAMPEAUX

(b. *c.* 1070, Champeaux, France—d. 1121, Châlons-sur-Marne)

William of Champeaux was a French bishop, logician, theologian, and philosopher who was prominent in the Scholastic controversy on the nature of universals.

After studies under the polemicist Manegold of Lautenbach in Paris, the theologian Anselm of Laon, and the philosopher Roscelin at Compiègne, William taught in the cathedral school of Notre Dame, Paris, where he had Peter Abelard among his pupils. He became head of the school and archdeacon of Paris in about 1100 but retired in 1108, probably because of the violent polemics, or controversial arguments, between him and Abelard over the doctrine of universals.

William withdrew to the nearby abbey of Saint-Victor, where—at the school he established with Anselm's aid— he taught rhetoric, logic, and theology, again having Abelard as his pupil. The abbey flourished under William's direction, contributing significantly to the mystical trend characteristic of Victor. He was consecrated bishop of Châlons-sur-Marne in 1113 and initiated a reform, becoming an advocate of clerical celibacy and a champion of orthodoxy and ecclesiastical investiture. In 1115 he ordained the great Bernard of Clairvaux, who probably studied under him.

William's surviving works are all theological; his logical works are not extant. His *Sententiae seu Quaestiones* ("Sentences or Questions") is an early systematization of classical Christian doctrine.

PETER ABELARD

(b. 1079, Le Pallet, near Nantes, Brittany [now in France]—d. April 21, 1142, Priory of Saint-Marcel, near Chalon-sur-Saône, Burgundy [now in France])

Peter Abelard was a French theologian and philosopher best known for his solution of the problem of universals

Peter Abelard, with Héloïse, miniature portrait by Jean de Meun, 14th century; in the Musee Conde, Chantilly, France. Courtesy of the Musée Condé, Chantilly, Fr.; photograph, Giraudon/Art Resource, New York

and for his original use of dialectics. He is also known for his poetry and for his celebrated love affair with Héloïse.

EARLY LIFE

The outline of Abelard's career is well known, largely because he described so much of it in his famous *Historia calamitatum* ("History of My Troubles"). He was born the son of a knight in Brittany south of the Loire River. He sacrificed his inheritance and the prospect of a military career in order to study philosophy, particularly logic, in France. He provoked bitter quarrels with two of his masters, Roscelin of Compiègne and William of Champeaux, who represented opposite poles of philosophy in regard to the question of the existence of universals. Roscelin was a nominalist who asserted that universals are nothing more than mere words; William in Paris upheld a form of Platonic realism according to which universals have an independent existence. Abelard in his own logical writings brilliantly elaborated an independent philosophy of language. While showing how words could be used significantly, he stressed that language itself is not able to demonstrate the truth of things (*res*) that lie in the domain of physics.

Abelard was a peripatetic both in the manner in which he wandered from school to school at Paris, Melun, Corbeil, and elsewhere and as one of the exponents of Aristotelian logic who were called the Peripatetics. In 1113 or 1114 he went north to Laon to study theology under Anselm of Laon, the leading biblical scholar of the day. He quickly developed a strong contempt for Anselm's teaching, which he found vacuous, and returned to Paris. There he taught openly but was also given as a private pupil the young Héloïse, niece of one of the clergy of the cathedral of Paris, Canon Fulbert. Abelard and Héloïse fell in love

Saint Denis Abbey, Seine Saint Denis, France. Manuel Cohen/Getty Images

and had a son whom they called Astrolabe. They then married secretly. To escape her uncle's wrath, Héloïse withdrew into the convent of Argenteuil outside Paris. Abelard suffered castration at Fulbert's instigation. In shame, he embraced the monastic life at the royal abbey of Saint-Denis near Paris and made the unwilling Héloïse become a nun at Argenteuil.

CAREER AS A MONK

At Saint-Denis, Abelard extended his reading in theology and tirelessly criticized the way of life followed by his fellow monks. His reading of the Bible and of the Church Fathers led him to make a collection of quotations that seemed to represent inconsistencies of teaching by the Christian church. He arranged his findings in a compilation entitled *Sic et non* ("Yes and No"); and for it he wrote a preface in which, as a logician and as a keen student of language, he formulated basic rules with which students might reconcile apparent contradictions of meaning and distinguish the various senses in which words had been used over the course of many centuries. He also wrote the first version of his book called *Theologia,* which was formally condemned as heretical and burned by a council held at Soissons in 1121. Abelard's dialectical analysis of the mystery of God and the Trinity was held to be erroneous, and he himself was placed for a while in the abbey of Saint-Médard under house arrest. When he returned to Saint-Denis he applied his dialectical methods to the subject of the abbey's patron saint; he argued that Denis of Paris, the martyred apostle of Gaul, was not identical with Dionysius the Areopagite, the convert of St. Paul. The monastic community of Saint-Denis regarded this criticism of their traditional claims as derogatory to the kingdom; and, in order to avoid being brought for trial before the king of France, Abelard fled from the abbey and sought asylum in the territory of Count Theobald of Champagne. There he sought the solitude of a hermit's life but was pursued by students who pressed him to resume his teaching in philosophy. His combination of the teaching of secular arts with his profession as a monk was heavily criticized by other men of religion, and Abelard contemplated flight outside Christendom altogether. In 1125, however, he accepted election as abbot of the remote Breton monastery of Saint-Gildas-de-Rhuys. There, too, his relations with the community deteriorated, and, after attempts had been made upon his life, he returned to France.

Héloïse had meanwhile become the head of a new foundation of nuns called the Paraclete. Abelard became the abbot of the new community and provided it with a rule and with a justification of the nun's way of life; in this he emphasized the virtue of literary study. He also provided books of hymns he had composed, and in the early 1130s he and Héloïse composed a collection of their own love letters and religious correspondence.

FINAL YEARS

About 1135 Abelard went to the Mont-Sainte-Geneviève outside Paris to teach, and he wrote in a blaze of energy and of celebrity. He produced further drafts of his *Theologia* in which he analyzed the sources of belief in the Trinity and praised the pagan philosophers of classical antiquity for their virtues and for their discovery by the use of reason of many fundamental aspects of Christian revelation. He also wrote a book called *Ethica* or *Scito te ipsum* ("Know

Thyself"), a short masterpiece in which he analyzed the notion of sin and reached the drastic conclusion that human actions do not make a person better or worse in the sight of God, for deeds are in themselves neither good nor bad. What counts with God is a person's intention; sin is not something done (it is not *res*); it is uniquely the consent of a human mind to what it knows to be wrong. Abelard also wrote *Dialogus inter philosophum, Judaeum et Christianum* ("Dialogue Between a Philosopher, a Jew, and a Christian") and a commentary on Paul's Letter to the Romans, the *Expositio in Epistolam ad Romanos,* in which he outlined an explanation of the purpose of Christ's life, which was to inspire people to love him by example alone.

The tombs of Abelard and Héloïse, Père-Lachaise Cemetery, Paris, Ile-De-France. DEA/G. Dagli Orti/De Agostini/Getty Images

On the Mont-Sainte-Geneviève, Abelard drew crowds of pupils, many of them men of future fame, such as the English humanist John of Salisbury. He also, however, aroused deep hostility in many by his criticism of other masters and by his apparent revisions of the traditional teachings of Christian theology. At a council held at Sens in 1140, Abelard underwent a resounding condemnation, which was soon confirmed by Pope Innocent II. He withdrew to the great monastery of Cluny in Burgundy. There, under the skillful mediation of the abbot, Peter the Venerable, he made peace with Bernard of Clairvaux and retired from teaching. Now both sick and old, he lived the life of a Cluniac monk. After his death, his body was first sent to the Paraclete; it now lies alongside that of Héloïse in the cemetery of Père-Lachaise in Paris. Epitaphs composed in his honour suggest that Abelard impressed some of his contemporaries as one of the greatest thinkers and teachers of all time.

WILLIAM OF SAINT-THIERRY

(b. c. 1085, Liège, Lower Lorraine—d. probably Sept. 8, 1148)

William of Saint-Thierry was a French monk, theologian, and mystic and a leading adversary of early medieval rationalistic philosophy.

William studied under Anselm of Laon, a supporter of the philosophical theology (later called Scholasticism) advanced by Anselm of Canterbury. After entering a Benedictine abbey in Reims in 1113, William became thoroughly versed in scriptural and patristic writings. Elected abbot of the Abbey of Saint-Thierry, near Reims, in 1119, he expressed his preference for contemplation and writing rather than ecclesiastical administration, but he remained in office at the urging of his friend Bernard of

Clairvaux. During that period William wrote two works fundamental to his theological system, *De natura et dignitate amoris* ("On the Nature and Dignity of Love") and *De contemplando Deo* ("On the Contemplation of God"). *De sacramento altaris* ("On the Sacrament of the Altar"), a treatise on the Eucharist, he dedicated to Bernard, who earlier had dedicated two of his own works to William.

From 1128 to 1135 William compiled several treatises and biblical commentaries attempting to synthesize the theology and mysticism of Western and Eastern Christianity, specifically an integration of the thought of Augustine, Origen, and Gregory of Nyssa. William's *Meditativae orationes* ("Meditative Prayers") expressed spiritual concerns with an intensity comparable to Augustine's in his *Confessions*. In 1135 he withdrew to the meditative life of the Cistercian Monastery of Signy in the Ardennes, where he addressed questions of the spiritual life and the problem of faith in his *Speculum fidei* (*The Mirror of Faith*) and *Aenigma fidei* ("The Enigma of Faith"), written in 1144. In the same year, after visiting the Charterhouse of Mont-Dieu, near Reims, he composed the *Epistola ad fratres de Monte Dei* ("Letter to the Brothers of Mont-Dieu"), called the "Golden Epistle," one of the most significant medieval works on the value of the contemplative life.

Elaborating the essential elements of his doctrine on mysticism, William proposed that the soul, although alienated from God, is also intrinsically empowered to experience a mystical "return" to its divine origin during its earthly existence, a return effected in stages. Thus are humans progressively liberated from their material and temporal impediments, eventually undergoing an experiential knowledge of God by a process of reminiscence, understanding, and love.

St. Bernard of Clairvaux, detail of an altar piece by the Florentine School, early 15th century; in the Staatliche Museen zu Berlin. Courtesy of the Staatliche Museen zu Berlin, Germany

SAINT BERNARD OF CLAIRVAUX

(b. 1090, probably Fontaine-les-Dijon, near Dijon, Burgundy—d. Aug. 20, 1153, Clairvaux, Champagne)

Bernard of Clairvaux was a Cistercian monk and mystic, the founder and abbot of the Abbey of Clairvaux and one of the most influential churchmen of his time.

EARLY LIFE AND CAREER

Born of Burgundian landowning aristocracy, Bernard grew up in a family of five brothers and one sister. The familial atmosphere engendered in him a deep respect for mercy, justice, and loyal affection for others. Faith and morals were taken seriously, but without priggishness. Both his parents were exceptional models of virtue. It is said that his mother, Aleth, exerted a virtuous influence upon Bernard only second to what Monica had done for Augustine in the 5th century. Her death, in 1107, so affected Bernard that he claimed that this is when his "long path to complete conversion" began. He turned away from his literary education, begun at the school at Châtillon-sur-Seine, and from ecclesiastical advancement, toward a life of renunciation and solitude.

Bernard sought the counsel of the abbot of Cîteaux, Stephen Harding, and decided to enter this struggling, small, new community that had been established by Robert of Molesmes in 1098 as an effort to restore Benedictinism to a more primitive and austere pattern of life. Bernard took his time in terminating his domestic affairs and in persuading his brothers and some 25 companions to join him. He entered the Cîteaux community in 1112, and from then until 1115 he cultivated his spiritual and theological studies.

Bernard's struggles with the flesh during this period may account for his early and rather consistent penchant for physical austerities. He was plagued most of his life by impaired health, which took the form of anemia, migraine, gastritis, hypertension, and an atrophied sense of taste.

FOUNDER AND ABBOT OF CLAIRVAUX

In 1115 Stephen Harding appointed him to lead a small group of monks to establish a monastery at Clairvaux, on the borders of Burgundy and Champagne. Four brothers, an uncle, two cousins, an architect, and two seasoned monks under the leadership of Bernard endured extreme deprivations for well over a decade before Clairvaux was self-sufficient. Meanwhile, as Bernard's health worsened, his spirituality deepened. Under pressure from his ecclesiastical superiors and his friends, notably the bishop and scholar William of Champeaux, he retired to a hut near the monastery and to the discipline of a quack physician. It was here that his first writings evolved. They are characterized by repetition of references to the Church Fathers and by the use of analogues, etymologies, alliterations, and biblical symbols, and they are imbued with resonance and poetic genius. It was here, also, that he produced a small but complete treatise on Mariology (study of doctrines and dogmas concerning the Virgin Mary), "Praises of the Virgin Mother." Bernard was to become a major champion of a moderate cult of the Virgin, though he did not support the notion of Mary's immaculate conception.

By 1119 the Cistercians had a charter approved by Pope Calixtus II for nine abbeys under the primacy of the abbot of Cîteaux. Bernard struggled and learned to live with the inevitable tension created by his desire to serve others in charity through obedience and his desire to cultivate his inner life by remaining in his monastic enclosure. His more than 300 letters and sermons manifest his quest to combine a mystical life of absorption in God with his friendship for those in misery and his concern for the faithful execution of responsibilities as a guardian of the life of the church.

It was a time when Bernard was experiencing what he apprehended as the divine in a mystical and intuitive manner. He could claim a form of higher knowledge that is the complement and fruition of faith and that reaches completion in prayer and contemplation. He could also commune with nature and say:

> *Believe me, for I know, you will find something far greater in the woods than in books. Stones and trees will teach you that which you cannot learn from the masters.*

After writing a eulogy for the new military order of the Knights Templar he would write about the fundamentals of the Christian's spiritual life, namely, the contemplation and imitation of Christ, which he expressed in his sermons "The Steps of Humility" and "The Love of God."

PILLAR OF THE CHURCH

The mature and most active phase of Bernard's career occurred between 1130 and 1145. In these years both Clairvaux and Rome, the centre of gravity of medieval Christendom, focussed upon Bernard. Mediator and counsellor for several civil and ecclesiastical councils and for theological debates during seven years of papal disunity, he nevertheless found time to produce an extensive number of sermons on the Song of Solomon. As the confidant of five popes, he considered it his role to assist in healing the church of wounds inflicted by the antipopes (those elected pope contrary to prevailing clerical procedures), to oppose the rationalistic influence of the greatest and most popular dialectician of the age, Peter Abelard, and to cultivate the friendship of the greatest churchmen of the time. He could also rebuke a pope, as he did in his letter to Innocent II:

> *There is but one opinion among all the faithful shepherds among us, namely, that justice is vanishing in the Church, that the power of the keys is gone, that episcopal authority is altogether turning rotten while not a bishop is able to avenge the wrongs done to God, nor is allowed to punish any misdeeds whatever, not even in his own diocese (parochia). And the cause of this they put down to you and the Roman Court.*

Bernard's confrontations with Abelard ended in inevitable opposition because of their significant differences of temperament and attitudes. In contrast with the tradition of "silent opposition" by those of the school of monastic spirituality, Bernard vigorously denounced dialectical Scholasticism as degrading God's mysteries, as one technique among others, though tending to exalt itself above the alleged limits of faith. One seeks God by learning to live in a school of charity and not through "scandalous curiosity," he held. "We search in a worthier manner, we discover with greater facility through prayer than through disputation." Possession of love is the first condition of the knowledge of God. However, Bernard finally claimed a victory over Abelard, not because of skill or cogency in argument but because of his homiletical denunciation and his favoured position with the bishops and the papacy.

Pope Eugenius III and King Louis VII of France induced Bernard to promote the cause of a Second Crusade (1147–49) to quell the prospect of a great Muslim surge engulfing both Latin and Greek Orthodox Christians. The crusade ended in failure because of Bernard's inability to account for the quarrelsome nature of politics, peoples, dynasties, and adventurers. He was an idealist with the ascetic ideals of Cîteaux grafted upon those of his father's knightly tradition and his mother's piety, who read into the hearts of the crusaders—many of whom were bloodthirsty fanatics—his own integrity of motive.

In his remaining years he participated in the condemnation of Gilbert de La Porrée—a scholarly dialectician and bishop of Poitiers who held that Christ's divine nature was only a human concept. He exhorted Pope Eugenius to stress his role as spiritual leader of the church over his role as leader of a great temporal power, and he was a major figure in church councils. His greatest literary endeavour, "Sermons on the Canticle of Canticles," was written during this active time. It revealed his teaching, often described as "sweet as honey," as in his later title *doctor mellifluus,* given to him by Pope Pius XII in 1953. It was a love song supreme: "The Father is never fully known if He is not loved perfectly." Add to this one of Bernard's favourite prayers, "Whence arises the love of God? From God. And what is the measure of this love? To love without measure," and one has a key to his doctrine. Bernard was declared a doctor of the church in 1830.

SAINT HILDEGARD

(b. 1098, Böckelheim, West Franconia [Germany]—d. Sept. 17, 1179, Rupertsberg, near Bingen)

Hildegard, also known as Hildegard of Bingen, was a German abbess, visionary mystic, and composer.

Hildegard was born of noble parents and was educated at the Benedictine cloister of Disibodenberg by Jutta, an anchorite and sister of the count of Spanheim. Hildegard was 15 years old when she began wearing the Benedictine habit and pursuing a religious life. She succeeded Jutta as prioress in 1136. Having experienced visions since she was a child, at age 43 she consulted her confessor, who in turn reported the matter to the archbishop of Mainz. A committee of theologians subsequently confirmed the authenticity of Hildegard's visions, and a monk was appointed to help her record them in writing. The finished work, *Scivias* (1141–52), consists of 26 visions that are prophetic and apocalyptic in form and in their treatment of such topics as the church, the relationship between God and humanity, and redemption. About 1147 Hildegard left Disibodenberg with several nuns to found a new convent at Rupertsberg, where she continued to exercise the gift of prophecy and to record her visions in writing.

A talented poet and composer, Hildegard collected 77 of her lyric poems, each with a musical setting composed by her, in *Symphonia armonie celestium revelationum*. Her numerous other writings include lives of saints; two treatises on medicine and natural history, reflecting a quality of scientific observation rare at that period; and extensive correspondence, in which are to be found further prophecies and allegorical treatises. She also for amusement contrived her own language. She traveled widely throughout Germany, evangelizing to large groups of people about her visions and religious insights. Although her earliest biographer proclaimed her a saint and miracles were reported during her life and at her tomb, she was never formally canonized. She is, however, listed as a saint in the Roman Martyrology and is honoured on her feast day in certain German dioceses.

ISAAC OF STELLA

(b. *c.* 1100, England—d. *c.* 1169, Étoile, near Poitiers, Aquitaine, France)

Isaac of Stella was a monk, philosopher, and theologian, a leading thinker in 12th-century Christian humanism, and

Hildegard of Bingen. Hulton Archive/Getty Images

a proponent of a synthesis of Neoplatonic and Aristotelian philosophies.

After studies in England and Paris, Isaac entered the abbey of Cîteaux, near Dijon, in the midst of the Cistercian monastic reform carried out by Bernard of Clairvaux. In 1147 Isaac was elected abbot of Étoile, a Cistercian community. Several years later, he attempted to found a monastery on l'Île (island) de Ré, near the French port of La Rochelle. There he composed a series of Lenten conferences that proposed a proof for God's existence by arguing from the insufficiency of created things and also submitted a theory of atonement. The addresses reflected not only the logical method of Anselm of Canterbury but also adopted notions from the 5th-century Latin and Greek Neoplatonism of Augustine and Pseudo-Dionysius.

Returning to Étoile, Isaac later composed his principal work, the *Epistola de anima ad Alcherum* ("Letter to Alcher on the Soul"), a compendium of psychology in the Cistercian tradition of providing a logical basis for theories of mysticism, done in 1162 at the request of the monk-philosopher Alcher of Clairvaux. This treatise served as the basis for the celebrated medieval tract *De spiritu et anima* ("On the Spirit and the Soul"), long believed to have been Augustine's but now attributed by some scholars to Alcher.

The *Epistola de anima* integrates Aristotelian and Neoplatonic psychological theories with Christian mysticism. In the Platonic tradition, Isaac considers the hierarchical order of reality—body, soul, God—in ascending order of knowability and advances the tripartite division of the soul—viz., rational, appetitive, and emotional functions. His theory of knowledge, however, includes the Aristotelian view of five forms of sense perception, of memory and imagination, and of a reasoning power that abstracts universal concepts from the images of individual objects. The intellect, or the capacity to grasp eternal ideas in time, and the intelligence that enables humans to intuit the reality of God exhibit further Neoplatonic orientation. The influence of mysticism appears in his suggestion that the highest level of knowledge depends on the intervention of divine illumination and in his *via negativa* ("way of negation") for knowing God—viz., the reality of God is the negation of every material and human quality. Unexcelled in his grasp of Neoplatonism, Isaac interpreted biblical texts in a philosophical perspective.

PETER LOMBARD

(b. *c.* 1100, Novara, Lombardy [Italy]—d. Aug. 21/22, 1160, Paris, France)

Peter Lombard was a bishop of Paris whose *Sententiarum libri IV* (1148–51; *Four Books of Sentences*) was the standard theological text of the Middle Ages.

After early schooling at Bologna, he went to France to study at Reims and then at Paris. From 1136 to 1150 he taught theology in the school of Notre Dame, Paris, where in 1144–45 he became a canon—i.e., staff clergyman. Lombard was present at the Council of Reims (1148) that assembled to examine the writings of the French theologian Gilbert de La Porrée. In June 1159 he was consecrated bishop of Paris and died the following year.

Although he wrote sermons, letters, and commentaries on Holy Scripture, Lombard's *Four Books of Sentences* established his reputation and subsequent fame, earning him the title of *magister sententiarum* ("master of the sentences"). The *Sentences,* a collection of teachings of the Church Fathers and opinions of medieval masters arranged as a systematic treatise, marked the culmination of a long tradition of theological pedagogy, and until the 16th century it was the official textbook in the universities. Hundreds of scholars wrote commentaries on it, including the celebrated philosopher Aquinas.

Book I of the *Sentences* discusses God, the Trinity, divine guidance, evil, predestination; Book II, angels, demons, the Fall of man, grace, sin; Book III, the Incarnation of Jesus Christ, the redemption of sins, virtues, the Ten Commandments; Book IV, the sacraments and the four last things—death, judgment, hell, and heaven. While Lombard showed originality in choosing and arranging his texts, in utilizing different currents of thought, and in avoiding extremes, of special importance to medieval theologians was his clarification of the theology of the sacraments. He asserted that there are seven sacraments and that a sacrament is not merely a "visible sign of invisible grace" (after Augustine) but also the "cause of the grace it signifies." In ethical matters, he decreed that a person's actions are judged good or bad according to their cause and intention, except those acts that are evil by nature.

Lombard's teachings were opposed during his lifetime and after his death. Later theologians rejected a number of his views, but he was never regarded as unorthodox, and efforts to have his works condemned were unsuccessful. The fourth Lateran Council (1215) approved his teaching on the Trinity and prefaced a profession of faith with the words "We believe with Peter Lombard."

THIERRY OF CHARTRES

(b. *c.* 1100, France—d. *c.* 1150, Chartres, France)

Thierry of Chartres was a French theologian, teacher, and encyclopaedist and one of the foremost thinkers of the 12th century.

According to Peter Abelard, Thierry attended the Council of Soissons in 1121, at which Abelard's teachings were condemned. He taught at Chartres, where his brother Bernard of Chartres, a celebrated Platonist, was chancellor. Sometime after 1136 he began teaching in Paris, where he had the Latinist, John of Salisbury, among his pupils. In 1141 he became archdeacon and chancellor of Chartres. After attending the Diet of Frankfurt in 1149, he later retired to a monastic life.

Thierry's unpublished *Heptateuchon* ("Book in Seven Volumes") contains the "classics" of the seven liberal arts, including works by Cicero on rhetoric and by Aristotle on logic. His cosmology, mainly expounded in his commentary on Genesis, attempts to harmonize Scripture with Platonic and other physical or metaphysical doctrines; it teaches that God—who is everything—is the ultimate form from which all other forms were created. In the Latin West, he was among the first to promote the Arabian knowledge of science, thus contributing to that important movement beginning in the 11th century in which Eastern science was—through Latin translations of Arabic works—introduced into the West, where science had disappeared with the Latin Roman Empire.

WILLIAM OF CONCHES

(b. *c.* 1100, Conches, France—d. 1154)

William of Conches was a French Scholastic philosopher and a leading member of the School of Chartres.

A pupil of Bernard of Chartres, he taught at Chartres and Paris and was tutor to Henry (later Henry II of England), son of Geoffrey Plantagenet.

William, a realist whose ideas leaned toward pantheism, gave an atomistic explanation of nature, the four elements (air, water, fire, earth) being regarded as combinations of homogeneous individual atoms. He wrote explanations of Plato's *Timaeus* and Boethius's *Consolation of Philosophy* and composed two original works, *Philosophia Mundi* ("Philosophy of the World") and *Pragmaticon Philosophiae* ("The Business of Philosophy"). He is also considered to be the author of the *Summa Moralium Philosophorum* ("The Substance of the Ethical Philosophies"), the earliest medieval treatise on ethics.

GERARD OF CREMONA

(b. *c.* 1114, Cremona, Lombardy [Italy] — d. 1187, Toledo, kingdom of Castile [Spain])

Gerard of Cremona was a European medieval scholar who translated the works of many major Greek and Arabic writers into Latin.

Gerard went to Toledo to learn Arabic in order to read the *Almagest* of the 2nd-century-CE Greek mathematician and astronomer Ptolemy, which was not then available in Latin; he remained there for the rest of his life. About 80 translations from the Arabic have been attributed to him, but it has been suggested that he was in charge of a school of translators that was responsible for some of the translations. Many early printed editions omit the name of the translator. Gerard's translation of the *Almagest* (printed in 1515) was finished in 1175. Among other Greek authors translated from Arabic versions by Gerard (according to tradition) are Aristotle, Euclid, and Galen. Translations of original Arabic texts attributed to him include works on medicine—notably the *Canon* of Avicenna—mathematics, astronomy, astrology, and alchemy.

JOHN OF SALISBURY

(b. 1115/20, Salisbury, Wiltshire, Eng.—d. Oct. 25, 1180, probably at Chartres, France)

John of Salisbury was one of the best Latinists of his age. He was secretary to Theobald and Thomas Becket, archbishops of Canterbury, and became bishop of Chartres.

After 1135 he attended cathedral schools in France for 12 years and studied under Peter Abelard (1136). He was a clerk in Theobald's household in 1148 and during the next five years was mainly employed by the archbishop on missions to the Roman Curia. His *Historia pontificalis* (c. 1163) gives a vivid description of the papal court during this period, partly through its character sketches. From 1153 John's main duty was to draft the archbishopric's official correspondence with the Curia, especially in connection with appeals. In the late summer of 1156 this activity angered King Henry II, who regarded him as a champion of ecclesiastical independence.

The crisis passed, but to some extent it influenced John's two books, the *Policraticus* and the *Metalogicon* (both 1159), in which his general intention was to show his contemporaries that in their thought and actions they were defecting from the true task of humanity. His work represented a protest against the professional specialization slowly developing in royal and papal administration and in the universities. He unfavourably contrasted the way of life followed by courtiers and administrators with an ideal practice derived from Latin poets and from classical and patristic writers.

Out of favour with Henry, John was exiled to France (1163) shortly before Becket was exiled. From his refuge in the monastery of Saint-Rémi at Reims, John wrote many letters assessing the prospects of the Canterbury case.

After the reconciliation of Henry and Becket, he returned to England (1170) and was in Canterbury Cathedral when Becket was assassinated (Dec. 29, 1170). Thereafter, John was occupied with collecting Becket's correspondence and preparing a biographical introduction. He became bishop of Chartres in 1176 and took an active part in the third Lateran Council (March 1179). He was buried at Chartres.

GODFREY OF SAINT-VICTOR

(b. *c.* 1125—d. 1194, Paris, France)

Godfrey of Saint-Victor was a French monk, philosopher, theologian, and poet whose writings summarized an early medieval Christian humanism that strove to classify areas of knowledge, to integrate distinctive methods of learning, and to recognize the intrinsic dignity of humanity and nature.

A student with the arts faculty at Paris, Godfrey was influenced early by dialectical thought. After a brief period of teaching, in about 1160 he entered the Augustinian abbey of Saint-Victor, Paris, where he further developed his cultural humanism. An unsympathetic monastic superior, however, harassed Godfrey to such an extent that he was obliged to leave the abbey in about 1180 for the solitude of a rural priory. There he wrote his principal work, *Microcosmus.* After the superior's death (*c.* 1190), he returned permanently to Saint-Victor.

The central theme of *Microcosmus* recalls the insight of classical philosophy and of the early Church Fathers— viz., that the human individual is a microcosm, containing in himself the material and spiritual elements of reality. *Microcosmus* offers one of the first attempts by a medieval Scholastic philosopher to systematize history and knowledge into a comprehensive, rational structure. Godfrey used the symbolism of a biblical framework to treat the physical, psychological, and ethical aspects of human beings. He affirmed the matter-spirit unity in humans and the basic goodness of human nature, tempering this optimism with the realization that human nature has been weakened ("fractured") by sin, but not to an intrinsically corrupted and irreparable extent.

Godfrey admits four principal capabilities in humans: sensation, imagination, reason, and intelligence. Humans' analytic reason and power of insight have the theoretical science of philosophy for their natural fulfillment. But a supernatural fulfillment, he maintains, consists in love. To this end divine intervention is needed to confer on humans the perfective graces, or gifts, of enlightenment, affectivity, and perseverance.

In his other notable work, the *Fons philosophiae* (c. 1176; "The Fount of Philosophy"), Godfrey, in rhymed verse, proposed a classification of learning and considered the controversy between realists and nominalists over the problem of universals. *Fons philosophiae* is an allegorical account of the sources of Godfrey's intellectual formation (e.g., Plato, Aristotle, and Boethius), symbolized as a flowing stream from which he drew water as a student.

Another treatise, "Anatomy of the Body of Christ," appended to *Fons philosophiae,* is a leading example of medieval Christian symbolism. A long poem ascribing to each member and organ of Christ's body some aspect of humans' natural and supernatural purpose, it assembled texts from the early Church Fathers and helped form medieval devotion to the humanity of Christ. Godfrey's writings have won appreciation as a prime example of 12th-century humanism, although their fundamental concepts of the positive values of humans and nature were recognized to a limited extent by the high Scholasticism of the 13th century.

JOACHIM OF FIORE

(b. *c.* 1130, Celico, Kingdom of Naples [Italy]—d. 1201/02, Fiore)

Joachim of Fiore was an Italian mystic, theologian, biblical commentator, philosopher of history, and founder of the monastic order of San Giovanni in Fiore. He developed a philosophy of history according to which history develops in three ages of increasing spirituality: the ages of the Father, the Son, and the Holy Spirit.

The known facts regarding the life of Joachim of Fiore are few. Legends about his parentage and youth are of little historical significance, but from an autobiographical reference it seems certain that he went on a pilgrimage to the Holy Land that reputedly had an effect on his conversion to the religious life. He became a Cistercian monk at Sambucina and in 1177 abbot of Corazzo (Sicily). About 1191 he broke away from the distracting duties of administration and retired into the mountains to follow the contemplative life. Although claimed as a fugitive by the Cistercians, Joachim was allowed by Pope Celestine III to form the disciples who gathered around him at San Giovanni in Fiore (a town located in present-day Cosenza province in Calabria) into the Order of San Giovanni in Fiore in 1196.

Far more significant is the evidence for the inner development of a man who came to believe that spiritual understanding would be given to one who wrestled with the "letter" of the Scriptures to get at the "spirit." Three moments of special illumination are indicated, but the first is known only in legendary form, connected with either his pilgrimage or his novitiate at Sambucina. The second, recorded by himself, took place one Easter eve, after a period of frustrated study of the biblical book of Revelation when he felt himself "imprisoned" by difficulties. In the midnight silence, suddenly his mind was flooded with clarity and his understanding released from prison. The third was an experience at Pentecost, when, after a time of agonizing doubt on the doctrine of the Trinity, Joachim had a vision of a psaltery with 10 strings, in a triangular form, that clarified the mystery through a visual symbol and called forth paeans of praise from him. He expresses this experience of illumination given after mental striving in terms of the city seen intermittently by the approaching pilgrim or of the spirit breaking through the hard rind of the letter.

He was summoned by Pope Lucius III in 1184 and urged to press on with the biblical exegesis he had begun. This probably refers to the *Liber concordie Novi ac Veteris Testamenti* ("Book of Harmony of the New and Old Testaments"), in which Joachim worked out his philosophy of history, primarily in a pattern of "twos"— the concords between the two great dispensations (or Testaments) of history, the Old and the New. But already Joachim's spiritual experience was creating in his mind his truly original "pattern of threes." If the *spiritualis intellectus* springs from the letter of the Old and New Testaments, then history itself must culminate in a final age of the spirit that proceeds from both the previous ages. Thus was born his trinitarian philosophy of history in which the three Persons are, as it were, built into the time structure in the three ages or *status* of the Father, Son, and Holy Spirit.

The third *status* was to be won by the church only after arduous pilgrimage and great tribulation, like the Israelites marching through the wilderness and crossing the Jordan River into the Promised Land. As guides through this crucial stage, Joachim prophesied the advent of two new orders of spiritual persons, one of hermits to agonize for the world on the mountaintop and one a mediating order to lead others on to the new spiritual plane. Although the third age belongs par excellence to contemplatives, secular clergy and laypersons are not shut out of it. In a strange diagram, a "ground plan" of the New Jerusalem, various categories of monks are grouped around the seat of God, but below, secular clergy and tertiaries (lay members) live according to their rule.

In the *Expositio in Apocalypsim* ("Exposition of the Apocalypse"), Joachim seeks to probe the imminent crisis of evil, as pictured in the apocalyptic symbols of the Antichrist, and the life of the spirit to follow. His third main work, the *Psalterium decem chordarum* ("Psaltery of Ten Strings"), expounds his doctrine of the Trinity through the symbol of his vision of the 10-stringed psaltery. Here and in a lost tract he attacked the doctrine of "quaternity" (an overemphasis on the "one essence" of the Godhead that seems to separate it from the three Persons of the Trinity and so create a fourth), which he attributed to Peter Lombard. Besides this trilogy, written concurrently, Joachim left minor tracts and one uncompleted major work, the *Tractatus super quattuor Evangelia* ("Treatise on the Four Gospels").

Joachim was a poet and artist. His lyricism breaks through the biblical exegesis that he chose as his medium and the turgid Latin of his style. Above all, his visual imagination is expressed in the unique *Liber figurarum* ("Book of Figures"; discovered in 1937), a book of drawings and figures thought to be a genuine work by most Joachim scholars today. Here his vision of the culminating age of history is embodied in trees that flower and bear fruit luxuriantly at the top; his doctrine of the Trinity is expressed in remarkable geometric figures; his kaleidoscopic vision fuses images in some strange shapes, such as the tree that becomes an eagle, which may have influenced Dante. Joachim's figures probably carried his ideas in exciting and popular form far more widely than his indigestible writings.

In his lifetime Joachim was acclaimed as a prophet, gifted with divine illumination, and this is how he was seen by the first chroniclers after his death. The condemnation of his tract against Peter Lombard by the fourth Lateran Council in 1215 dimmed his reputation for a time, but the appearance of the Franciscan and Dominican mendicant orders, hailed as Joachim's new spiritual men, reestablished him as a prophet. The Spiritual Franciscans at mid-13th century and various other friars, monks, and sects down to the 16th century appropriated his prophecy of a third age. But Joachim has always had a double reputation, as saint and as heretic, for cautious Christian thinkers and leaders have seen his writings as highly dangerous.

HUGH OF SAINT-VICTOR

(b. 1096 — d. Feb. 11, 1141, Paris, France),

Hugh of Saint-Victor was an eminent scholastic theologian who began the tradition of mysticism that made the school of Saint-Victor, Paris, famous throughout the 12th century.

Of noble birth, Hugh joined the Augustinian canons at the monastery of Hamersleben, near Halberstadt (now in Germany). He went to Paris (c. 1115) with his uncle, Archdeacon Reinhard of Halberstadt, and settled at Saint-Victor Abbey. From 1133 until his death, the school of Saint-Victor flourished under Hugh's guidance.

His mystical treatises were strongly influenced by Augustine, whose practical teachings on contemplative life Hugh blended with the theoretical writings of Pseudo-Dionysius. Hugh's somewhat innovative style of exegesis made an important contribution to the development of

Hugh of Saint-Victor, undated engraving. Library of Congress, Washington, D.C. (digital file no. 3c05618)

natural theology: he based his arguments for God's existence on external and internal experience and added a teleological proof originating from the facts of experience. His chief work on dogmatic theology was *De sacramentis Christianae fidei* ("The Sacraments of the Christian Faith"), which anticipated some of the works of Aquinas.

Unlike some of his contemporaries, Hugh upheld secular learning by promoting knowledge as an introduction to contemplative life: "Learn everything," he said, "and you will see afterward that nothing is useless." A prolific writer, Hugh wrote the *Didascalicon,* a remarkably comprehensive early encyclopaedia, as well as commentaries on the Scriptures and on the *Celestial Hierarchy* of Pseudo-Dionysius.

WILLIAM OF AUXERRE

(b. *c.* 1150, Auxerre, Bishopric of Auxerre [France]—d. Nov. 3, 1231, Rome [Italy])

William of Auxerre was a French philosopher and theologian who contributed to the adaptation of classical Greek philosophy to Christian doctrine. He is considered the first medieval writer to develop a systematic treatise on free will and the natural law.

Probably a student of Richard of Saint-Victor, William became a master in theology and later an administrator at the University of Paris. After a long career at the university, he was commissioned in 1230 to serve as French envoy to Pope Gregory IX to advise Gregory on dissension at the university. William pleaded the cause of the students against the complaints of King Louis IX.

In 1231 William was appointed by Gregory to a three-member council to censor the works of Aristotle included in the university curriculum to make them conform sufficiently to Christian teaching. Contrary to the papal legate Robert of Courçon and other conservatives, who in 1210 condemned Aristotle's *Physics* and *Metaphysics* as corruptive of Christian faith, William saw no intrinsic reason to avoid the rational analysis of Christian revelation. Confident of William's orthodoxy, Gregory urged Louis to restore him to the university faculty so that he and Godfrey of Poitiers might reorganize the plan of studies. William fell ill and died before any of these projects were begun.

William's principal work is the *Summa super quattuor libros sententiarum* ("Compendium on the Four Books of Sentences"), usually called the *Summa aurea* ("The Golden Compendium"), a commentary on early and medieval Christian theological teachings assembled by Peter Lombard in the mid-12th century. Written between 1215 and 1220, the *Summa aurea,* in four books, selectively treated such theological matters as God as one nature in three persons, creation, humanity, Christ and the virtues, sacramental worship, and the Last Judgment.

William's emphasis on philosophy as a tool for Christian theology is evidenced by his critique of Plato's doctrine of a demiurge, or cosmic intelligence, and by his treatment of the theory of knowledge as a means for distinguishing between God and creation. He also analyzed certain moral questions, including the problem of human choice and the nature of virtue.

William also wrote a *Summa de officiis ecclesiasticis* ("Compendium of Church Services"), which treated liturgical, or common, prayer, sacramental worship, and the annual cycle of scripture readings and chants. This systematic study served as the model for the late-13th-century noted work on divine worship, Guillaume Durand's *Rationale divinorum officiorum* ("An Explanation of the Divine Offices").

RICHARD OF SAINT-VICTOR

(b. Scotland/England—d. March 10, 1173, Paris, France)

Richard of Saint-Victor was a theologian whose treatises profoundly influenced both medieval and modern mysticism.

Richard entered the Abbey of Saint-Victor, Paris, and studied under the scholastic theologian and philosopher Hugh of Saint-Victor, becoming prior in 1162. Although Richard wrote on the Trinity and the Scriptures, he is chiefly remembered for his works on mysticism. With their extensive symbolism, his works synthesize and elaborate the teachings that made the school of Saint-Victor renowned throughout the 12th century.

According to Richard, the soul proceeds from sense perception to ecstasy through imagination, reason, and intuition. The soul employs secular learning as well as divine revelation until it is finally united with God in divine contemplation. Richard's *Benjamin major* and *Benjamin minor* became standard manuals on the practice of mystical spirituality.

His influence on medieval mysticism is evident in the works of the 13th-century Italian theologian Bonaventure, who discussed faith as the foundation of mystical contemplation in the tradition of the school of Saint-Victor, and in those of the 14th-century French theologian Jean de Gerson. Richard's influence on later mysticism is evidenced by the appearance of six editions of his works between 1506 and 1650.

CHAPTER 3

ARABIC AND JEWISH
THOUGHT

In the 11th and 12th centuries, a cultural revolution took place that influenced the entire subsequent history of Western philosophy. The old style of education, based on the liberal arts and emphasizing grammar and the reading of the Latin classics, was replaced by the new methods of Scholasticism, which stressed logic and dialectic. John of Salisbury (c. 1115–1180), of the School of Chartres, witnessed this radical change:

> *Behold, everything was being renovated: grammar was being made over, logic was being remodeled, rhetoric was being despised. Discarding the rules of their predecessors, [the masters] were teaching the quadrivium with new methods taken from the very depths of philosophy.*

In philosophy itself, there was a decline in Platonism and a growing interest in Aristotelianism. This change was occasioned by the translation into Latin of the works of Aristotle, which had earlier been translated into Arabic by Arab philosophers. Until the appearance of these works in Latin, only a few of Aristotle's minor logical treatises were known by European philosophers. With the translation of major works such as the *Topics,* the *Prior Analytics,* and *Posterior Analytics,* Scholastic philosophers gained access to Aristotelian methods of disputation and science, which became their own techniques of discussion and inquiry. Many other philosophical and scientific works of Greek and Arabic origin were translated at this time, creating a "knowledge explosion" in western Europe.

Among the works to be translated from Arabic were some of the writings of the Iranian philosopher Avicenna (980–1037), who had an extraordinary impact on the medieval Schoolmen. His interpretation of Aristotle's notion of metaphysics as the science of *ens qua ens* (Latin: "being as being"), his analysis of many metaphysical terms, such as *being, essence,* and *existence,* and his metaphysical proof of the existence of God were often quoted, with approval or disapproval, in Christian circles. Also influential were his psychology, logic, and natural philosophy. His *Al-Qānūn fī al-ṭibb* (*Canon of Medicine*) was authoritative on the subject until modern times. The *Maqāṣid al-falāsifah* (1094; "The Aims of the Philosophers") of the Arab theologian al-Ghazālī (1058–1111), an exposition of Avicenna's philosophy written in order to criticize it, was read as a complement to Avicenna's works. The anonymous *Liber de causis* ("Book of Causes") was also translated into Latin from Arabic. This work, excerpted from *Stiocheiōsis theologikē* (*Elements of Theology*), by the Greek philosopher Proclus (*c.* 410–485), was often ascribed to Aristotle, and it gave a Neoplatonic cast to his philosophy until its true origin was discovered by Aquinas.

The commentaries of the Arabic philosopher Averroës (1126–98) were translated along with Aristotle's works. As Aristotle was called "the Philosopher" by European philosophers, Averroës was dubbed "the Commentator." The Christian Schoolmen often attacked Averroës as the archenemy of Christianity for his rationalism and his doctrine of the eternity of the world and the unity of the intellect

for all human beings—i.e., the doctrine that intellect is a
single, undifferentiated form with which individuals
become reunited at death. This was anathema to the
Christian Schoolmen because it contravened the Christian
doctrine of individual immortality.

Of considerably less influence on the Scholastics was
medieval Jewish thought. Ibn Gabirol (*c.* 1022–*c.* 1058), known
to the Scholastics as Avicebron or Avencebrol, was thought
to be an Arab or Christian, though in fact he was a Spanish
Jew. His chief philosophical work, written in Arabic and
preserved in toto only in a Latin translation titled *Fons vitae*
(*c.* 1050; *The Fountain of Life*), stresses the unity and simplicity of God. All creatures are composed of form and matter,
either the gross corporeal matter of the sensible world or
the spiritual matter of angels and human souls. Some of the
Schoolmen were attracted to the notion of spiritual matter
and also to Ibn Gabirol's analysis of a plurality of forms in
creatures, according to which every corporeal being receives
a variety of forms by which it is given its place in the hierarchy of being—for example, a dog has the forms of a
corporeal thing, a living thing, an animal, and a dog.

Moses Maimonides (1135–1204), or Moses ben Maimon,
was known to Christians of the Middle Ages as Rabbi
Moses. His *Dalālat al-hā'irīn* (*c.* 1190; *The Guide for the
Perplexed*) helped them to reconcile Greek philosophy
with revealed religion. For Maimonides there could be no
conflict between reason and faith because both come
from God; an apparent contradiction is due to a misinter-
pretation of either the Bible or the philosophers. Thus, he
showed that creation is reconcilable with philosophical
principles and that the Aristotelian arguments for an eternal world are not conclusive because they ignore the
omnipotence of God, who can create a world of either
finite or infinite duration.

The remainder of this chapter will discuss in detail the lives, work, and influence of the great Arabic and Jewish philosophers of the Middle Ages.

AVICENNA

(b. 980, near Bukhara, Iran [now in Uzbekistan]—d. 1037, Hamadan)

Avicenna was the most famous and influential of the philosopher-scientists of Islam. He was particularly noted for his contributions in the fields of Aristotelian philosophy and medicine. In addition to his famous *Al-Qānūn fī al-ṭibb*

Avicenna. National Library of Medicine

(*Canon of Medicine*), he composed the *Kitāb al-shifā'* (*Book of Healing*), a vast philosophical and scientific encyclopaedia.

LIFE

Avicenna, an ethnic Persian who spent his whole life in the eastern and central regions of Iran, received his earliest education in Bukhara under the direction of his father. Since the house of his father was a meeting place for learned men, from his earliest childhood Avicenna was able to profit from the company of the outstanding masters of his day. A precocious child with an exceptional memory that he retained throughout his life, he had memorized the Qur'ān and much Arabic poetry by the age of 10. Thereafter, he studied logic and metaphysics under teachers whom he soon outgrew and then spent the few years until he reached the age of 18 in his own self-education. He read avidly and mastered Islamic law, then medicine, and finally metaphysics. Particularly helpful in his intellectual development was his gaining access to the rich royal library of the Sāmānids—the first great native dynasty that arose in Iran after the Arab conquest—as the result of his successful cure of the Sāmānid prince Nūḥ ibn Manṣūr. By the time he was 21, he was accomplished in all branches of formal learning and had already gained a wide reputation as an outstanding physician. His services were also sought as an administrator, and for a while he even entered government service as a clerk.

But suddenly the whole pattern of his life changed. His father died; the Sāmānid house was defeated by Maḥmūd of Ghazna, the Turkish leader and legendary hero who established Ghaznavid rule in Khorāsān (northeastern Iran and modern western Afghanistan); and Avicenna began a period of wandering and turmoil, which was to last to the end of his life with the exception of a few unusual intervals of tranquillity. Destiny had plunged Avicenna into one of the tumultuous periods of Iranian history, when new Turkish elements were replacing Iranian domination in Central Asia and local Iranian dynasties were trying to gain political independence from the 'Abbāsid caliphate in Baghdad (in modern Iraq). But the power of concentration and the intellectual prowess of Avicenna was such that he was able to continue his intellectual work with remarkable consistency and continuity and was not at all influenced by the outward disturbances.

Avicenna wandered for a while in different cities of Khorāsān and then left for the court of the Būyid princes, who were ruling over central Iran, first going to Rayy (near modern Tehrān) and then to Qazvīn, where as usual he made his livelihood as a physician. But in these cities also he found neither sufficient social and economic support nor the necessary peace and calm to continue his work. He went, therefore, to Hamadan in west-central Iran, where Shams al-Dawlah, another Būyid prince, was ruling. This journey marked the beginning of a new phase in Avicenna's life. He became court physician and enjoyed the favour of the ruler to the extent that twice he was appointed vizier. As was the order of the day, he also suffered political reactions and intrigues against him and was forced into hiding for some time; at one time he was even imprisoned.

The last phase of Avicenna's life began with his move to Eṣfahān (about 250 miles south of Tehrān). In 1022 Shams al-Dawlah died, and Avicenna, after a period of difficulty that included imprisonment, fled to Eṣfahān with a small entourage. In Eṣfahān, Avicenna was to spend the last 14 years of his life in relative peace. He was esteemed highly by 'Alā' al-Dawlah, the ruler, and his court. Accompanying 'Alā' al-Dawlah on a campaign, Avicenna fell ill and, despite his attempts to treat himself, died from colic and from exhaustion.

THE "ORIENTAL PHILOSOPHY"

Avicenna's personal philosophical views, he said, were those of the ancient sages of Greece (including the genuine views of Plato and Aristotle), which he had set forth in the "Oriental Philosophy," a book that has not survived and probably was not written or meant to be written. They were not identical with the common Peripatetic (Aristotelian) doctrines and were to be distinguished from the learning of his contemporaries, the Christian "Aristotelians" of Baghdad, which he attacked as vulgar, distorted, and falsified. His most voluminous writing, *The Book of Healing*, was meant to accommodate the doctrines of other philosophers as well as hint at his own personal views, which are elaborated elsewhere in more imaginative and allegorical forms.

DISTINCTION BETWEEN ESSENCE AND EXISTENCE AND THE DOCTRINE OF CREATION

Avicenna had learned from certain hints in al-Fārābī (c. 878–c. 950) that the exoteric teachings of Plato regarding "forms," "creation," and the immortality of individual souls were closer to revealed doctrines than were the genuine views of Aristotle; that the doctrines of Plotinus and later Neoplatonic commentators were useful in harmonizing Aristotle's views with revealed doctrines; and that philosophy must accommodate itself to the divine law on the issue of creation and of reward and punishment in the hereafter, which presupposes some form of individual immortality. Following al-Fārābī's lead, Avicenna initiated a full-fledged inquiry into the question of being, in which he distinguished between essence and existence. He argued that the fact of existence cannot be inferred from or accounted for by the essence of existing things and that form and matter by themselves cannot interact and originate the movement of the universe or the progressive actualization of existing things. Existence must, therefore, be due to an agent-cause that necessitates, imparts, gives, or adds existence to an essence. To do so, the cause must be an existing thing and coexist with its effect. The universe consists of a chain of actual beings, each giving existence to the one below it and responsible for the existence of the rest of the chain below. Because an actual infinite is deemed impossible by Avicenna, this chain as a whole must terminate in a being that is wholly simple and one, whose essence is its very existence, and therefore is self-sufficient and not in need of something else to give it existence. Because its existence is not contingent on or necessitated by something else but is necessary and eternal in itself, it satisfies the condition of being the necessitating cause of the entire chain that constitutes the eternal world of contingent existing things.

All creation is necessarily and eternally dependent upon God. It consists of the intelligences, souls, and bodies of the heavenly spheres, each of which is eternal, and the sublunary sphere, which is also eternal, undergoing a perpetual process of generation and corruption, of the succession of form over matter, very much in the manner described by Aristotle.

THE IMMORTALITY OF INDIVIDUAL SOULS

There is, however, a significant exception to this general rule: the human rational soul. As a human being, the individual can affirm the existence of his soul from direct consciousness of his self (what he means when he says "I"); and he can imagine this happening even in the absence of external objects and bodily organs. This proves, according to Avicenna, that the soul is an indivisible, immaterial, and incorruptible substance, not imprinted in matter, but created with the body, which it uses as an instrument. Unlike other immaterial substances (the intelligences and souls of the spheres), it is not pre-eternal but is generated, or made to exist, at the same time as the individual body—which can receive it—is formed. The composition, shape, and disposition of its body and the soul's success or failure in managing and controlling it, the formation of moral habits, and the acquisition of knowledge all contribute to its individuality and difference from other souls. Although the body is not resurrected after its corruption, the soul survives and retains all the individual characteristics, perfections or imperfections, that it achieved in its earthly existence and in this sense is rewarded or punished for its past deeds. Avicenna's claim that he has presented a philosophical proof for the immortality of generated ("created") individual souls no doubt constitutes the high point of his effort to harmonize philosophy and religious beliefs.

PHILOSOPHY, RELIGION, AND MYSTICISM

Having accounted for the more difficult issues of creation and the immortality of individual souls, Avicenna proceeded to explain the faculty of prophetic knowledge (the "sacred" intellect), revelation (imaginative representation meant to convince the multitude and improve their earthly life), miracles, and the legal and institutional arrangements (acts of worship and the regulation of personal and public life) through which the divine law achieves its end. Avicenna's explanation of almost every aspect of Islam is pursued on the basis of extensive exegesis of the Qur'ān and the Ḥadīth. The primary function of religion is to assure the happiness of the many. This practical aim of religion (which Avicenna saw in the perspective of Aristotle's practical science) enabled him to appreciate the political and moral functions of divine revelation and to account for its form and content. Revealed religion, however, has a subsidiary function also—that of indicating to the few the need to pursue the kind of life and knowledge appropriate to rare individuals endowed with special gifts. These persons must be dominated by the love of God to facilitate the achievement of the highest knowledge. In many places Avicenna appears to identify such people with the mystics. The identification of the philosopher as a kind of mystic conveyed a new image of the philosopher as a member of the religious community who is distinguished from his coreligionists by his other-worldliness, dedicated to the inner truth of religion, and consumed by the love of God.

Avicenna's allegorical and mystical writings are usually called "esoteric" in the sense that they contain his personal views cast in an imaginative, symbolic form. The esoteric works must, then, be interpreted. Their interpretation must move away from the explicit doctrines contained in "exoteric" works such as the *Shifā'* and recover "the unmixed and uncorrupted truth" set forth in the "Oriental Philosophy." The Oriental Philosophy, however, has never been available to anyone, and, as noted above, it is doubtful that it was written at all. This dilemma has made interpretation both difficult and rewarding for Muslim philosophers and modern scholars alike.

AVICENNA'S INFLUENCE

In the Western world, Avicenna's influence was felt, though no distinct school of "Latin Avicennism" can be discerned as can with Averroës. The *Book of Healing* was translated partially into Latin in the 12th century, and the complete *Canon* appeared in the same century. These translations and others spread the thought of Avicenna far and wide in the West. His thought, blended with that of Augustine, was a basic ingredient in the thought of many of the medieval Scholastics, especially in the Franciscan schools. In medicine the *Canon* became the unparalleled medical authority for several centuries, and Avicenna enjoyed an undisputed place of honour equaled only by the early Greek physicians Hippocrates and Galen. In the East his dominating influence in medicine, philosophy, and theology has lasted over the ages and is still alive within the circles of Islamic thought.

AL-GHAZĀLĪ

(b. 1058, Ṭūs, Iran—d. Dec. 18, 1111, Ṭūs)

Al- Ghazālī was an Islamic theologian and mystic whose great work, *Iḥyāʾ ʿulūm ad-dīn* ("The Revival of the Religious Sciences"), made Ṣūfism (Islamic mysticism) an acceptable part of orthodox Islam.

Al-Ghazālī was educated at Ṭūs, his birthplace, then in Jorjān, and finally at Nishapur (Neyshābūr), where his teacher was al-Juwaynī, who earned the title of *imām al-ḥaramayn* (the imam of the two sacred cities of Mecca and Medina). After the latter's death in 1085, al-Ghazālī was invited to go to the court of Niẓām al-Mulk, the powerful vizier of the Seljuq sultans. The vizier was so impressed by al-Ghazālī's scholarship that in 1091 he appointed him chief professor in the Niẓāmīyah college in Baghdad. While lecturing to more than 300 students, al-Ghazālī was also mastering and criticizing the Neoplatonist philosophies of al-Fārābī and Avicenna. He passed through a spiritual crisis that rendered him physically incapable of lecturing for a time. In November 1095 he abandoned his career and left Baghdad on the pretext of going on pilgrimage to Mecca. Making arrangements for his family, he disposed of his wealth and adopted the life of a poor Ṣūfī, or mystic. After some time in Damascus and Jerusalem, with a visit to Mecca in November 1096, al-Ghazālī settled in Ṭūs, where Ṣūfī disciples joined him in a virtually monastic communal life. In 1106 he was persuaded to return to teaching at the Niẓāmīyah college at Nishapur. A consideration in this decision was that a "renewer" of the life of Islam was expected at the beginning of each century, and his friends argued that he was the "renewer" for the century beginning in September 1106. He continued lecturing in Nishapur at least until 1110, when he returned to Ṭūs, where he died the following year.

More than 400 works are ascribed to al-Ghazālī, but he probably did not write nearly so many. Frequently, the same work is found with different titles in different manuscripts, but many of the numerous manuscripts have not yet been carefully examined. Several works have also been falsely ascribed to him, and others are of doubtful authenticity. At least 50 genuine works are extant.

Al-Ghazālī's greatest work is *Iḥyā' 'ulūm ad-dīn*. In 40 "books" he explained the doctrines and practices of Islam and showed how these can be made the basis of a profound devotional life, leading to the higher stages of Ṣūfism, or mysticism. The relation of mystical experience to other forms of cognition is discussed in *Mishkāt al-anwār* (*The Niche for Lights*). Al-Ghazālī's abandonment of his career and adoption of a mystical, monastic life is defended in the autobiographical work *al-Munqidh min aḍ-ḍalāl* (*The Deliverer from Error*).

His philosophical studies began with treatises on logic and culminated in the *Tahāfut* (*The Inconsistency—or*

Incoherence—of the Philosophers), in which he defended Islam against such philosophers as Avicenna, who sought to demonstrate certain speculative views contrary to accepted Islamic teaching. In preparation for this major treatise, he published an objective account of *Maqāsid al-falāsifah* (*The Aims of the Philosophers*—i.e., their teachings). This book was influential in Europe and was one of the first to be translated from Arabic to Latin (12th century).

Most of his activity was in the field of jurisprudence and theology. Toward the end of his life he completed a work on general legal principles, *al-Mustasfā* (*Choice Part, or Essentials*). His compendium of standard theological doctrine (translated into Spanish), *al-Iqtisād fī al-l 'tiqād* (*The Just Mean in Belief*), was probably written before he became a mystic, but there is nothing in the authentic writings to show that he rejected these doctrines, even though he came to hold that theology—the rational, systematic presentation of religious truths—was inferior to mystical experience. From a similar standpoint he wrote a polemical work against the militant sect of the Assassins (Ismāʿīlīyah), and he also wrote (if it is authentic) a criticism of Christianity, as well as *Nasīhat al-mulūk* (*Counsel for Kings*).

AVERROËS

(b. 1126, Córdoba [Spain]—d. 1198, Marrakech, Almohad empire [now in Morocco])

The Arabic philosopher who exerted the greatest influence over the development of European philosophy during the Middle Ages was Averroës. His series of summaries and commentaries on most of Aristotle's works (1169–95) and on Plato's *Republic* shaped the interpretation

A detail of the Mezquita in Cordoba, Spain. This World Heritage Site was a mosque until Cordoba was captured by Christian forces in the 13th century.
© www.istockphoto.com / brytta

of philosophers both in the Islamic world and in Europe for centuries. He wrote the *Faṣl al-Maḳāl* (*Decisive Treatise on the Agreement Between Religious Law and Philosophy*), the *Kashf al-Manāhij* (*Examination of the Methods of Proof Concerning the Doctrines of Religion*), and the *Tahāfut al-Tahāfut* (*The Incoherence of the Incoherence*), all in defense of the philosophical study of religion against the theologians (1179–80). He died at Marrakech, the North African capital of the Almohad dynasty.

EARLY LIFE

Averroës was born into a distinguished family of jurists at Córdoba and died at Marrakech, the North African capital of the Almohad dynasty. Thoroughly versed in the traditional Muslim sciences (especially exegesis of the Qur'ān—Islamic scripture—and Ḥadīth, or traditions, and *fiqh,* or law), trained in medicine, and accomplished in philosophy, Averroës rose to be chief *qāḍī* (judge) of Córdoba, an office also held by his grandfather (of the same name) under the Almoravids. After the death of the philosopher Ibn Ṭufayl, Averroës succeeded him as personal physician to the caliphs Abū Yaʿqūb Yūsuf in 1182 and his son Abū Yūsuf Yaʿqūb in 1184.

At some point between 1153 and 1169, Ibn Ṭufayl had introduced Averroës to Abū Yaʿqūb, who, himself a keen student of philosophy, frightened Averroës with a question concerning whether the heavens were created or not. The caliph answered the question himself, put Averroës at ease, and sent him away with precious gifts after a long conversation that proved decisive for Averroës' career. Soon afterward Averroës received the ruler's request to provide a badly needed correct interpretation of the philosophy of the Greek philosopher Aristotle, a task to which he devoted many years of his busy life as judge, beginning at Sevilla (Seville) and continuing at Córdoba. The exact year of his appointment as chief *qāḍī* of Córdoba, one of the key posts in the government (and not confined to the administration of justice), is not known.

COMMENTARIES ON ARISTOTLE

Between 1169 and 1195, Averroës wrote a series of commentaries on most of Aristotle's works. He wrote summaries, and middle and long commentaries—often two or all three kinds on the same work. Aristotle's *Politics* was inaccessible to Averroës; therefore he wrote a *Commentary on Plato's Republic*. All of Averroës' commentaries are incorporated in the Latin version of Aristotle's complete works. They are extant in the Arabic original or Hebrew translations or both, and some of these translations serve in place of the presumably lost Arabic originals—for example, the important commentaries on Aristotle's *Nicomachean Ethics* and on Plato's *Republic*.

Averroës' commentaries exerted considerable influence on Jews and Christians in the following centuries. His clear, penetrating mind enabled him to present competently Aristotle's thought and to add considerably to its understanding. He ably and critically used the classical commentators Themistius and Alexander of Aphrodisias and the Muslim philosophers al-Fārābī, Avicenna, and his own countryman Ibn Bājjah. In commenting on Aristotle's treatises on the natural sciences, Averroës showed considerable power of observation.

AVERROËS' DEFENSE OF PHILOSOPHY

Averroës' own first work is *Kulliyāt* (*General Medicine*), written between 1162 and 1169. Only a few of his legal writings and none of his theological writings are preserved.

Undoubtedly his most important writings are three closely connected religious-philosophical polemical treatises, composed in the years 1179 and 1180: the *Decisive Treatise on the Agreement Between Religious Law and Philosophy,* with its appendix; the *Examination of the Methods of Proof Concerning the Doctrines of Religion*; and the *Incoherence of the Incoherence,* in defense of philosophy. In the first two works, Averroës stakes a bold claim: only the metaphysician employing certain proof (syllogism) is capable and competent (as well as obliged) to interpret the doctrines contained in the prophetically revealed law (Sharī'ah), and not the Islamic *mutakallimūn* (dialectic theologians), who rely on dialectical arguments. To establish the true, inner meaning of religious beliefs and convictions is the aim of philosophy in its quest for truth. This inner meaning must not be divulged to the masses, who must accept the plain, external meaning of scripture contained in stories, similes, and metaphors. Averroës applied Aristotle's three arguments (demonstrative, dialectical, and persuasive— i.e., rhetorical and poetical) to the philosophers, the theologians, and the masses. The third work is devoted to a defense of philosophy against his predecessor al-Ghazālī's telling attack directed against Avicenna. Spirited and successful as Averroës' defense was, it could not restore philosophy to its former position, quite apart from the fact that the atmosphere in Muslim Spain and North Africa was most unfavourable to the unhindered pursuit of speculation. As a result of the reforming activity of Ibn Tūmart (c. 1078–1130), aimed at restoring pure monotheism, power was wrested from the ruling Almoravids, and the new Berber dynasty of the Almohads was founded, under whom Averroës served. In jurisprudence the emphasis then shifted from the practical application of Islamic law by appeal to previous authority to an equal stress on the study of its principles and the revival of independent legal decisions on the basis of Ibn Tūmart's teaching. Of perhaps even more far-reaching significance was Ibn Tūmart's idea of instructing the heretofore ignorant masses in the plain meaning of the Sharī'ah so that practice would be informed with knowledge. These developments were accompanied by the encouragement of the *falāsifah*—"those who," according to Averroës' *Decisive Treatise,* "follow the way of speculation and are eager for a knowledge of the truth"—to apply demonstrative arguments to the interpretation of the theoretical teaching of the Sharī'ah. But with the hands of both jurists and theologians thus strengthened, Averroës' defense of philosophy continued to be conducted within an unfavourable atmosphere.

Averroës himself acknowledged the support of Abū Ya'qūb, to whom he dedicated his *Commentary on Plato's Republic.* Yet Averroës pursued his philosophical quest in the face of strong opposition from the *mutakallimūn,* who, together with the jurists, occupied a position of eminence and of great influence over the fanatical masses. This may explain why he suddenly fell from grace when Abū Yūsuf— on the occasion of a jihad (holy war) against Christian Spain—dismissed him from high office and banished him to Lucena in 1195. To appease the theologians in this way at a time when the caliph needed the undivided loyalty and support of the people seems a more convincing reason than what the Arabic sources tell us (attacks on Averroës by the mob, probably at the instigation of jurists and theologians). But Averroës' disgrace was only short-lived— though long enough to cause him acute suffering—since the caliph recalled Averroës to his presence after his return to Marrakech. After his death, Averroës was first buried at Marrakech, and later his body was transferred to the family tomb at Córdoba.

Averroës. Hulton Archive/Getty Images

It is not rare in the history of Islam that the rulers' private attachment to philosophy and their friendship with philosophers goes hand in hand with official disapproval of philosophy and persecution of its adherents, accompanied by the burning of their philosophical writings and the prohibition of the study of secular sciences other than those required for the observance of the religious law. Without caliphal encouragement Averroës could hardly have persisted all his life in his fight for philosophy against the theologians, as reflected in his *Commentary on Plato's Republic*, in such works as the *Decisive Treatise* and *Incoherence of the Incoherence*, and in original philosophical treatises (e.g., about the union of the active intellect with the human intellect). It is likely that the gradual estrangement of his two masters and patrons from Ibn Tūmart's theology and their preoccupation with Islamic law also helped him. That Averroës found it difficult to pursue his philosophical studies alongside the conscientious performance of his official duties he himself reveals in a few remarks scattered over his commentaries—e.g., in that on Aristotle's *On the Parts of Animals*.

CONTENTS AND SIGNIFICANCE OF WORKS

To arrive at a balanced appraisal of Averroës' thought it is essential to view his literary work as a whole. In particular, a comparison of his religious-philosophical treatises with his *Commentary on Plato's Republic* shows the basic unity of his attitude to the Sharī'ah dictated by Islam and therefore determining his attitude to philosophy, more precisely to the *nomos* (law) of Plato's philosopher-king. It will then become apparent that there is only one truth for Averroës, that of the religious law, which is the same truth that the metaphysician is seeking. The theory of the double truth was definitely not formulated by Averroës, but rather by his Latin followers, the Averroists. Nor is it justifiable to say that philosophy is for the metaphysician what religion is for the masses. Averroës stated explicitly and unequivocally that religion is for all three classes; that the contents of the Sharī'ah are the whole and only truth for all believers; and that religion's teachings about reward and punishment and the hereafter must be accepted in their plain meaning by the elite no less than by the masses. The philosopher must choose the best religion, which, for a Muslim, is Islam as preached by Muhammad, the last of the prophets, just as Christianity was the best religion at the time of Jesus, and Judaism at the time of Moses.

It is significant that Averroës could say in his *Commentary on Plato's Republic* that religious law and philosophy have the same aim and in the *Decisive Treatise* that "philosophy is the companion and foster-sister of the Sharī'ah." Accepting Aristotle's division of philosophy into theoretical (physics and metaphysics) and practical (ethics and politics), he finds that the Sharī'ah teaches both to perfection: abstract knowledge commanded as the perception of God, and practice—the ethical virtues the law enjoins (*Commentary on Plato's Republic*). In the *Incoherence of the Incoherence* he maintains that "the religious laws conform to the truth and impart a knowledge of those actions by which the happiness of the whole creation is guaranteed." There is no reason to question the sincerity of Averroës. These statements reflect the same attitude to law and the same emphasis on happiness. Happiness as the highest good is the aim of political science. As a Muslim, Averroës insists on the attainment of happiness in this and the next life by all believers. This is, however, qualified by Averroës as the disciple of Plato: the highest intellectual perfection is reserved for the metaphysician, as in Plato's ideal state. But the Muslim's ideal state provides for the happiness of the masses as well because of its prophetically revealed law, which is superior to the Greek *nomos* for this reason. Averroës distinguishes between degrees of happiness and assigns every believer the happiness that corresponds to his intellectual capacity. He takes Plato to task for his neglect of the third estate because Averroës believes that everyone is entitled to his share of happiness. In his view, only the Sharī'ah of Islam cares for all believers. It legitimates speculation because it demands that the believer should know God. This knowledge is accessible to the naive believer in metaphors, the inner meaning of which is intelligible only to the metaphysician with the help of demonstration. On this point all *falāsifah* are agreed, and all recognize the excellence of the Sharī'ah stemming from its divinely revealed character. But only Averroës insists on its superiority over the *nomos*.

Insisting on the prerogative of the metaphysician—understood as a duty laid upon him by God—to interpret the doctrines of religion in the form of right beliefs and convictions (like Plato's philosopher-king), Averroës admits that the Sharī'ah contains teachings that surpass human understanding but that must be accepted by all believers because they contain divinely revealed truths. The philosopher is definitely bound by the religious law just as much as the masses and the theologians, who occupy a position somewhere in between. In his search for truth the metaphysician is bound by Arabic usage, as is the jurist in his legal interpretations, though the jurist uses subjective reasoning only, in contrast to the metaphysician's certain proof. This means that the philosopher is not bound to accept what is contradicted by demonstration. He can, thus, abandon belief in the creation out of nothing since Aristotle demonstrated the eternity of matter. Hence creation is a continuing process. Averroës sought justification for such an attitude in the fact that a

Muslim is bound only by consensus (*ijmāʿ*) of the learned in a strictly legal context where actual laws and regulations are concerned. Yet, since there is no consensus on certain theoretical statements, such as creation, he is not bound to conform. Similarly, anthropomorphism is unacceptable, and metaphorical interpretation of those passages in scripture that describe God in bodily terms is necessary. And the question whether God knows only the universals, but not the particulars, is neatly parried by Averroës in his statement that God has knowledge of particulars but that his knowledge is different from human knowledge. These few examples suffice to indicate that ambiguities and inconsistencies are not absent in Averroës' statements.

The *Commentary on Plato's Republic* reveals a side of Averroës that is not to be found in his other commentaries. While he carried on a long tradition of attempted synthesis between religious law and Greek philosophy, he went beyond his predecessors in spite of large-scale dependence upon them. He made Plato's political philosophy, modified by Aristotle, his own and considered it valid for the Islamic state as well. Consequently, he applied Platonic ideas to the contemporary Almoravid and Almohad states in a sustained critique in Platonic terms, convinced that if the philosopher cannot rule, he must try to influence policy in the direction of the ideal state. For Plato's ideal state is the best after the ideal state of Islam based on and centred in the Sharīʿah as the ideal constitution. Thus, he regrets the position of women in Islam compared with their civic equality in Plato's *Republic*. That women are used only for childbearing and the rearing of offspring is detrimental to the economy and responsible for the poverty of the state. This belief is most unorthodox.

Of greater importance is his acceptance of Plato's idea of the transformation and deterioration of the ideal, perfect state into the four imperfect states. Muʿāwiyah I, who in Islamic tradition perverted the ideal state of the first four caliphs into a dynastic power state, is viewed by Averroës in the Platonic sense as having turned the ideal state into a timocracy—a government based on love of honour. Similarly, the Almoravid and Almohad states are shown to have deteriorated from a state that resembled the original perfect Sharī'ah state into timocracy, oligarchy, democracy, and tyranny. Averroës here combines Islamic notions with Platonic concepts. In the same vein he likens the false philosophers of his time, and especially the *mutakallimūn,* to Plato's sophists. In declaring them a real danger to the purity of Islam and to the security of the state, he appeals to the ruling power to forbid dialectical theologians to explain their beliefs and convictions to the masses, thus confusing them and causing heresy, schism, and unbelief. The study of the *Republic* and the *Nicomachean Ethics* enabled the *falāsifah* to see more clearly the political character and content of the Sharī'ah in the context of the classical Muslim theory of the religious and political unity of Islam.

Leaning heavily on the treatment of Plato's political philosophy by al-Fārābī, Averroës looks at the *Republic* with the eyes of Aristotle, whose *Nicomachean Ethics* constitutes for Averroës the first, theoretical part of political science. He is, therefore, only interested in Plato's theoretical statements. Thus he concentrates on a detailed commentary on Books II–IX of the *Republic* and ignores Plato's dialectical statements and especially his tales and myths, principally the myth of Er. He explains Plato, whose *Laws* he also knows and uses, with the help, and in the light, of Aristotle's *Posterior Analytics, De anima* (*On the Soul*), *Physics,* and *Nicomachean Ethics.* Naturally, Greek pagan ideas and institutions are replaced by Islamic ones. Thus Plato's criticism of poetry (Homer) is applied to Arab pre-Islamic poetry, which he condemns.

Averroës sees much common ground between the Sharī'ah and Plato's general laws (interpreted with the help of Aristotle), notwithstanding his conviction that the Sharī'ah is superior to the *nomos*. He accepts al-Fārābī's equation of Plato's philosopher-king with the Islamic imam, or leader and lawgiver, but leaves it open whether the ideal ruler must also be a prophet. The reason for this may well be that as a sincere Muslim, Averroës holds that Muḥammad was "the seal of the prophets" who promulgated the divinely revealed Sharī'ah once and for all. Moreover, Averroës exempts Muḥammad from the general run of prophets, thus clearly rejecting the psychological explanation of prophecy through the theory of emanation adopted by the other *falāsifah*. No trace of this theory can be discovered in Averroës' writings, just as his theory of the intellect is strictly and purely Aristotelian and free from the theory of emanation.

In conclusion, it may be reiterated that the unity of outlook in Averroës' religious-philosophical writings and his *Commentary on Plato's Republic* gives his political philosophy a distinctly Islamic character and tone, thereby adding to his significance as a religious philosopher.

IBN GABIROL

(b. *c.* 1022, Málaga, caliphate of Córdoba—d. *c.* 1058/70, Valencia, kingdom of Valencia)

Ibn Gabirol was an important Neoplatonic philosopher and one of the outstanding figures of the Hebrew school of religious and secular poetry during the Jewish Golden Age in Moorish Spain. He received his higher education in Saragossa, where he joined the learned circle of other

Cordoban refugees established there around famed scholars and the influential courtier Yekutiel ibn Ḥasan.
Protected by this patron, whom Ibn Gabirol immortalized in poems of loving praise, the 16-year-old poet became
famous for his religious hymns in masterly Hebrew. The
customary language of Andalusian literature had been
Arabic, and Hebrew had only recently been revived as a
means of expression for Jewish poets. At 16 he could
rightly boast of being world famous:

> . . . *My song is a crown for kings and mitres on the heads of*
> *governors.*
> *My body walks upon the earth, while my spirit ascends to the*
> *clouds.*
> *Behold me: at sixteen my heart like that of a man of eighty is wise.*

He made, however, the mistake of lampooning Samuel
ha-Nagid, a rising Jewish statesman and vizier in the
Berber kingdom of Granada, who was also a talented poet,
Talmudist, strategist, and model writer of letters. After
making poetical amends, Ibn Gabirol seems to have been
admitted to the favour of this vizier, whose main court
encomiast he subsequently became.

This happened while the poet was involved (on the
Saragossan side) in the disproportionate strife between
the grammarians of Saragossa and those of Granada
concerning Hebrew linguistics. Being an emancipated
Cordoban, he offended the orthodox with heresies
such as recommending childlessness, denunciation of
the "world," Neoplatonism, and an almost insane self-
aggrandizement (coupled with the use of animal epithets
for his opponents). He apparently had to flee from
Saragossa; the circumstances leading to his departure are
described in his "Song of Strife":

Sitting among everybody crooked and foolish his [the poet's] heart only was wise.

The one slakes you with adder's poison, the other, flattering, tries to confuse your head.

One, setting you a trap in his design will address you: "Please, my lord."

A people whose fathers I would despise to be dogs for my sheep. . .

His "Song of Strife" and other poems show that his being a synagogal poet did not protect him against the hatred of his co-religionists in Saragossa, who called him a Greek because of his secular leanings.

Against all warnings by his patron Yekutiel, Ibn Gabirol concentrated on Neoplatonic philosophy, after having composed a non-offensive collection of proverbs in Arabic, *Mukhtār al-jawāhir* ("Choice of Pearls"), and a more original, though dated, ethical treatise (based on contemporary theories of the human temperaments), also in Arabic, *Kitāb islāḥ al-akhlāq* ("The Improvement of the Moral Qualities"). The latter contains chapters on pride, meekness, modesty, and impudence, which are linked with the sense of sight; and on love, hate, compassion, and cruelty, linked with hearing and other senses.

In need of a new patron after the execution of Yekutiel in 1039 by those who had murdered his king and taken over power, Ibn Gabirol secured a position as a court poet with Samuel ha-Nagid, who, becoming the leading statesman of Granada, was in need of the poet's prestige. Ibn Gabirol composed widely resounding poems with a messianic tinge for Samuel and for Jehoseph (Yūsuf), his son and later successor in the vizierate of Granada. All other biographical data about Ibn Gabirol except his place of death, Valencia, must be extrapolated from his poetry.

POETRY

The Jewish subculture of Moorish Andalusia (southern Spain) was engendered by the cultural "pressure" of the Arab peers. Ibn Gabirol's dual education, typical for the Jewish intelligentsia in the larger cities, must have encompassed both the entire Hebrew literary heritage— the Bible, Talmud, and other rabbinic writings and, in particular, Hebrew linguistics—and the Arabic, including the Qur'ān, Arabic secular and religious poetry and poetics, and the philosophical, philological, and possibly medical literature.

His poetry, like that of the entire contemporary Hebrew school, is modeled after the Arabic. Metrics, rhyme systems, and most of the highly developed imagery follow the Arabic school, but the biblical language adds a particular tinge. Many of Ibn Gabirol's poems show the influence of the knightly Arab bard al-Mutanabbī and the pessimistic Abū al-'Alā' al-Ma'arrī.

His secular topics included exaggerated, Arab-inspired self-praise, justified by the fame of the child prodigy; love poems (renouncing yet keenly articulate); praise of his noble and learned protectors, together with scathingly satirical reproach of others; dirges (the most moving of which are linked with the execution of the innocent Yekutiel); wine songs (sometimes libertine); spring and rain poems; flower portraits; the agonizingly realistic description of a skin ailment; and a long didactic poem on Hebrew grammar. Ibn Gabirol's long poetic description of a castle led to the discovery of the origins of the first Alhambra palace, built by the above-mentioned Jehoseph. Of a very rich production, about 200 secular poems and even more religious ones were preserved, though no collection of his poems survived. Many manuscript fragments of the former came to light only recently, preserved in synagogue attics by his co-religionists' respect for the Hebrew letter. Many of his religious poems were included in Jewish prayer books throughout the world.

His religious poems, in particular the poignant short prayers composed for the individual, presuppose the high degree of literacy typical of Moorish Spain, and they, too, show Arabic incentive. His famed rhymed prose poem "Keter malkhut" ("The Crown of the Kingdom"), a meditation stating the measurements of the spheres of the universe, jolts the reader into the abject feeling of his smallness but, subsequently, builds him up by a proclamation of the divine grace.

The following morning meditation exemplifies his religious poetry:

> *See me at dawn, my Rock; my Shelter, when my plight*
> *I state before Thy face likewise again at night,*
> *Outpouring anguished thought—that Thou behold'st my heart*
> *and what it contemplates I realise in fright.*
> *Low though the value be of mind's and lip's tribute*
> *to Thee (accomplishes aught my spirit with its might?).*
> *Most cherish'st Thou the hymn we sing before Thee. Thus,*
> *while Thou support'st my breath, I praise Thee in Thine height.*
> *Amen.*

PHILOSOPHY

His *Fountain of Life,* in five treatises, is preserved in toto only in the Latin translation, *Fons vitae,* with the author's name appearing as Avicebron or Avencebrol; it was re-identified as Ibn Gabirol's work in the 19th century. It had little influence upon Jewish philosophy other than on León Hebreo (Judah Abrabanel) and Benedict de Spinoza,

but it inspired the Kabbalists, the adherents of Jewish esoteric mysticism. Its influence upon Christian Scholasticism
was marked, although it was attacked by Aquinas for
equating concepts with realities. Grounded in Plotinus
and other Neoplatonic writers yet also in Aristotelian
logic and metaphysics, Ibn Gabirol developed a system in
which he introduced the conception of a divine will, like
the Logos (or divine "word") of Philo. It is an essential
unity of creativity of and with God, mutually related like
sun and sunlight, which mediates actively between the
transcendent deity and the cosmos that God created out
of nothingness (to be understood as the potentiality for
creation). Matter emanates directly from the deity as a
prime matter that supports all substances and even the
"intelligent" substances, the sphere-moving powers and
angels. This concept was accepted by the Franciscan
school of Scholastics but rejected by the Dominicans,
including Aquinas, for whom form (and only one, not
many) and not matter is the creative principle. Since matter, according to Aristotle and Plotinus, "yearns for
formation" and, thus, moving toward the nearness of God,
causes the rotation of the spheres, the finest matter of the
highest spheres is propelled by the strongest "yearning,"
which issues from God and returns to him and is active in
man (akin to the last line of Dante's *Divine Comedy:* "The
love which moves the sun and the other stars").

Yet, the dry treatise does not betray the passionate
quest of the Neoplatonist author. A philosophical poem,
beginning "That man's love," reveals the human intent.
Therein, a disciple asks the poet-philosopher what importance the world could have for the deity (to be understood
in Aristotelian terms as a deity that only contemplates its
own perfection). The poet answers that all of existence is
permeated, though to different degrees, by the yearning

of matter toward formation, and he declares that this yearning may give God the "glory" that the heavens proclaim, as the Bible teaches.

MOSES MAIMONIDES

(b. March 30, 1135, Córdoba [Spain]—d. Dec. 13, 1204, Egypt)

Moses Maimonides was the foremost intellectual figure of medieval Judaism. His first major work, begun at age 23 and completed 10 years later, was a commentary on the Mishna, the collected Jewish oral laws. A monumental code of Jewish law followed in Hebrew, *The Guide for the Perplexed* in Arabic, and numerous other works, many of major importance. His contributions in religion, philosophy, and medicine have influenced Jewish and non-Jewish scholars alike.

LIFE

Maimonides was born into a distinguished family. The young Moses studied with his learned father, Maimon, and other masters and at an early age astonished his teachers by his remarkable depth and versatility. Before Moses reached his 13th birthday, his peaceful world was suddenly disturbed by the ravages of war and persecution.

As part of Islamic Spain, Córdoba had accorded its citizens full religious freedom. But now the Islamic Mediterranean world was shaken by the Almohads, who captured Córdoba in 1148, leaving the Jewish community faced with the grim alternative of submitting to Islam or leaving the city. The Maimons temporized by practicing their Judaism in the privacy of their homes, while disguising their ways in public as far as possible to appear like

Muslims. They remained in Córdoba for some 11 years, and Maimonides continued his education in Judaic studies as well as in the scientific disciplines in vogue at the time.

When the double life proved too irksome to maintain in Córdoba, the Maimon family finally left the city about 1159 to settle in Fez, Morocco. Although it was also under Almohad rule, Fez was presumably more promising than Córdoba because there the Maimons would be strangers, and their disguise would be more likely to go undetected. Moses continued his studies in his favourite subjects, rabbinics and Greek philosophy, and added medicine to them. Fez proved to be no more than a short respite, however. In 1165 Rabbi Judah ibn Shoshan, with whom Moses had studied, was arrested as a practicing Jew and was found guilty and then executed. This was a sign to the Maimon family to move again, this time to Palestine, which was in a depressed economic state and could not offer them the basis of a livelihood. After a few months they moved again, now to Egypt, settling in Fostat, near Cairo. There Jews were free to practice their faith openly, although any Jew who had once submitted to Islam courted death if he relapsed to Judaism. Moses himself was once accused of being a renegade Muslim, but he was able to prove that he had never really adopted the faith of Islam and so was exonerated.

Although Egypt was a haven from harassment and persecution, Moses was soon assailed by personal problems. His father died shortly after the family's arrival in Egypt. His younger brother, David, a prosperous jewelry merchant on whom Moses leaned for support, died in a shipwreck, taking the entire family fortune with him, and Moses was left as the sole support of his family. He could not turn to the rabbinate because in those days the rabbinate was conceived of as a public service that did not offer its practitioners any remuneration. Pressed by

Moses Maimonides. Ken Welsh/Workbook Stock/Getty Images

economic necessity, Moses took advantage of his medical studies and became a practicing physician. His fame as a physician spread rapidly, and he soon became the court physician to the sultan Saladin, the famous Muslim military leader, and to his son al-Afḍal. He also continued a private practice and lectured before his fellow physicians at the state hospital. At the same time he became the leading member of the Jewish community, teaching in public and helping his people with various personal and communal problems.

Maimonides married late in life and was the father of a son, Abraham, who was to make his mark in his own right in the world of Jewish scholarship.

WORKS

The writings of Maimonides were numerous and varied. His earliest work, composed in Arabic at the age of 16, was the *Millot ha-Higgayon* ("Treatise on Logical Terminology"), a study of various technical terms that were employed in logic and metaphysics. Another of his early works, also in Arabic, was the *Essay on the Calendar* (Hebrew title: *Ma'amar ha'ibur*).

The first of Maimonides' major works, begun at the age of 23, was his commentary on the Mishna, *Kitāb al-Sirāj,* also written in Arabic. The Mishna is a compendium of decisions in Jewish law that dates from earliest times to the 3rd century. Maimonides' commentary clarified individual words and phrases, frequently citing relevant information in archaeology, theology, or science. Possibly the work's most striking feature is a series of introductory essays dealing with general philosophical issues touched on in the Mishna. One of these essays summarizes the teachings of Judaism in a creed of Thirteen Articles of Faith.

Medieval manuscript on vellum of the Mishneh Torah, a systematic code of Jewish law written by Maimonides. National Library, Jerusalem, Israel/ The Bridgeman Art Library/Getty Images

He completed the commentary on the Mishna at the age of 33, after which he began his magnum opus, the code of Jewish law, on which he also laboured for 10 years. Bearing the name of *Mishne Torah* ("The Torah Reviewed") and written in a lucid Hebrew style, the code offers a brilliant systematization of all Jewish law and doctrine. He wrote two other works in Jewish law of lesser scope: the *Sefer ha-mitzwot* (*Book of Precepts*), a digest of law for the less sophisticated reader, written in Arabic; and the *Hilkhot ha-Yerushalmi* ("Laws of Jerusalem"), a digest of the laws in the Palestinian Talmud, written in Hebrew.

His next major work, which he began in 1176 and on which he laboured for 15 years, was his classic in religious philosophy, the *Dalālat al-ḥā'irīn* (*The Guide for the Perplexed*), later known under its Hebrew title as the *Moreh nevukhim*. A plea for what he called a more rational philosophy of Judaism, it constituted a major contribution to the accommodation among science, philosophy, and religion. It was written in Arabic and sent as a private communication to his favourite disciple, Joseph ibn Aknin. The work was translated into Hebrew in Maimonides' lifetime and later into Latin and most European languages. It has exerted a marked influence on the history of religious thought.

Maimonides also wrote a number of minor works, occasional essays dealing with current problems that faced the Jewish community, and he maintained an extensive correspondence with scholars, students, and community leaders. Among his minor works those considered to be most important are *Iggert Teman* (*Epistle to Yemen*), *Iggeret ha-shemad* or *Ma'amar Qiddush ha-Shem* ("Letter on Apostasy"), and *Iggeret le-qahal Marsilia* ("Letter on Astrology," or, literally, "Letter to the Community of Marseille"). He also wrote a number of works dealing with medicine, including a popular miscellany of health rules, which he dedicated to the sultan al-Afḍal.

Maimonides complained often that the pressures of his many duties robbed him of peace and undermined his health. He died in 1204 and was buried in Tiberias, in the Holy Land, where his grave continues to be a shrine drawing a constant stream of pious pilgrims.

SIGNIFICANCE

Maimonides' advanced views aroused opposition during his lifetime and after his death. In 1233 one zealot, Rabbi Solomon of Montpellier, in southern France, instigated the church authorities to burn *The Guide for the Perplexed* as a dangerously heretical book. But the controversy abated after some time, and Maimonides came to be recognized as a pillar of the traditional faith—his creed became part of the orthodox liturgy—as well as the greatest of the Jewish philosophers.

Maimonides' epoch-making influence on Judaism extended also to the larger world. His philosophical work, translated into Latin, influenced the great medieval Scholastic writers, and even later thinkers, such as the Dutch-Jewish philosopher Benedict de Spinoza (1632–77) and the German rationalist philosopher and mathematician G.W. Leibniz (1646–1716), found in his work a source for some of their ideas. His medical writings constitute a significant chapter in the history of medical science.

CHAPTER 4

THE AGE OF THE SCHOOLMEN

While Western scholars were assimilating the treasures of Greek, Arabic, and Jewish thought, the universities that would become the centres of Scholasticism were being founded. Of these, the most important were located in Paris and Oxford (formed 1150–70 and 1168, respectively). "Scholasticism" is the name given to the theological and philosophical teachings of the Schoolmen in the universities. There was no single Scholastic doctrine, however, and for this reason it is difficult to define Scholastic philosophy beyond the generalization just offered. Each of the Scholastics developed his own doctrine, which was often in disagreement with that of his fellow teachers. They had in common a respect for the great writers of old, such as the Church Fathers, Aristotle, Plato, Boethius, Pseudo-Dionysius, Avicenna, and Averroës. These they called "authorities." Their interpretation and evaluation of the authorities, however, frequently differed. They also shared a common style and method that developed out of the teaching practices in the universities. Teaching was done by lecture and disputation (a formal debate). A lecture consisted of the reading of a prescribed text followed by the teacher's commentary on it. Masters also held disputations in which the affirmative and negative sides of a question

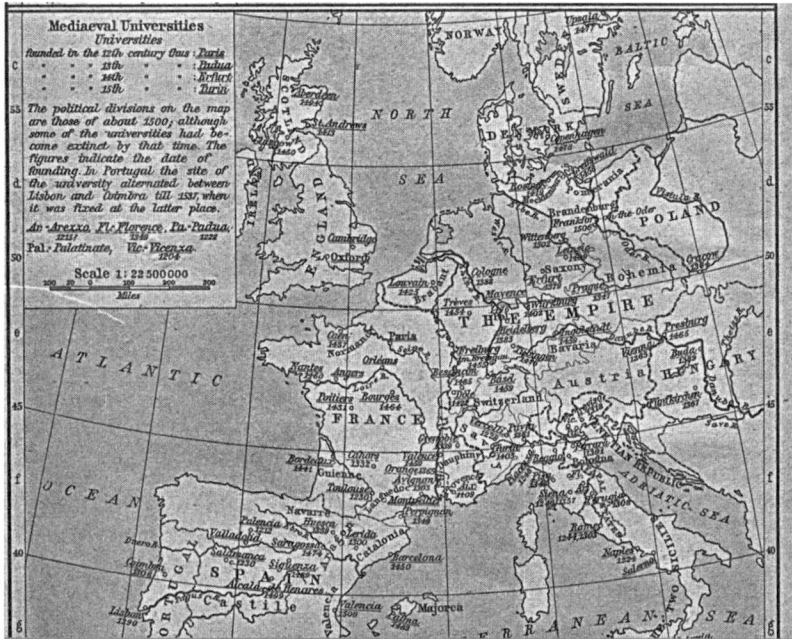

This map shows Europe's universities during the Medieval era. From The Historical Atlas by William R. Sheperd, 1923. Courtesy of the University of Texas Libraries, The University of Texas at Austin

were thoroughly argued by students and teacher before the latter resolved the problem.

THE NATURE OF SCHOLASTIC PHILOSOPHY

Scholasticism was so much a many-sided phenomenon that in spite of intensive research, scholars continue to differ considerably in their understanding of the term and in the emphases that they place on individual aspects of the phenomenon. Despite this lack of consensus, it is possible to provide a reasonably good characterization of the nature of Scholastic philosophy in general terms.

The traditional notion that Scholasticism was "school" philosophy—and, in fact, "Christian" school philosophy—can be understood only by examining the historical exigencies that created the need for schools. The search thus leads the inquirer back to the transition from antiquity to the Middle Ages—a point which, according to the great German philosopher Georg Wilhelm Friedrich Hegel (1770-1831), was marked by the symbolic date 529 CE, when a decree of the Christian emperor Justinian closed the Platonic Academy in Athens and sealed "the downfall of the physical establishments of pagan philosophy." In that same year, however, still another event occurred, which points much less to the past than to the coming age and, especially, to the rise of Scholasticism—viz., the foundation of Monte Cassino, the first Benedictine

The Benedictine monastery of Monte Cassino in Italy. Much of this monastery was destroyed during World War II, but was later rebuilt. Hulton Archive/Getty Images

abbey, above one of the highways of the great folk migra-
tions. This highly symbolic fact not only suggests the
initial shift of the scene of the intellectual life from places
like the Platonic Academy to the cloisters of Christian
monasteries, but it marks even more a change in the dra-
matis personae. New nations were about to overrun the
Roman Empire and its Hellenistic culture with long-
range effects: when, centuries later, for example, one of
the great Scholastics, Aquinas, was born, although he was
rightly a southern Italian, his mother was of Norman
stock, and his Sicilian birthplace was under central
European (Hohenstaufen) control.

It was a decisive and astonishing fact that the so-called
barbarian peoples who penetrated from the north into the
ancient world often became Christians and set out to master the body of tradition that they found, including the
rich harvest of patristic theology as well as the philosophical ideas of the Greeks and the political wisdom of the
Romans. This learning could be accomplished only in
the conquered empire's language (i.e., in Latin), which
therefore had to be learned first. In fact, the incorpora-
tion of both a foreign vocabulary and a different mode of
thinking and the assimilation of a tremendous amount
of predeveloped thought was the chief problem that
confronted medieval philosophy at its beginnings. And it
is only in the light of this fact that one of the decisive
traits of medieval Scholasticism becomes understandable:
Scholasticism above all was an unprecedented process
of learning, literally a vast "scholastic" enterprise that continued for several centuries. Since the existing material
had to be ordered and made accessible to learning and
teaching, the very prosaic labour and "schoolwork" of
organizing, sorting, and classifying materials inevitably
acquired an unprecedented importance. Consequently,
the writings of medieval Scholasticism quite naturally lack

the magic of personal immediacy, for schoolbooks leave little room for originality.

If the major historical task of that epoch was really to learn, to acquire, and to preserve the riches of tradition, a certain degree of "scholasticity" was not only inevitable but essential. It is not at all certain that today's historians would have direct intellectual access to Plato, Aristotle, and Augustine had the Scholastics not done their patient spadework. Besides, the progress from the stage of mere collection of given sentences and their interpretation (*expositio, catena, lectio*), to the systematic discussion of texts and problems (*quaestio, disputatio*), and finally to the grand attempts to give a comprehensive view of the whole of attainable truth (*summa*) was necessarily at the same time a clear progression toward intellectual autonomy and independence, which in order to culminate, as it did in the 13th century, in the great works of Scholasticism's Golden Age, required in addition the powers of genius, of philosophers like Albertus Magnus and Aquinas.

On the other hand, the moment had to come when the prevalent preoccupation with existing knowledge would give way to new questions, which demanded consideration and answers that could emerge only from direct experience. By the later Middle Ages, procedures for exploiting and discussing antecedent stocks of insight had been largely institutionalized, and it was an obvious temptation to perpetuate the dominion of those procedures—which could lead only to total sterility. It is widely agreed that this is almost exactly what did happen in the 14th century in what is called the "decline" and disintegration of Scholasticism.

THE MATURITY OF SCHOLASTICISM

By the turn of the 12th century, the world view of Western Christendom, on the whole Augustinian and Platonic in inspiration, was beginning to be rounded out into a system and to be institutionalized in the universities. At the very moment of its consolidation, however, an upheaval was brewing that would shake this novel conception to its foundations: the main works of Aristotle, hitherto unknown in the West, were being translated into Latin— among them his *Metaphysics,* the *Physics,* the *Nichomachean Ethics,* and the book *On the Soul.* These writings were not merely an addition of something new to the existing stock; they involved an enormous challenge. Suddenly, a new, rounded, coherent view of the world was pitted against another more-or-less coherent traditional view; and because this challenge bore the name of Aristotle, it could not possibly be ignored, for Aristotle's books on logic, translated and equipped with commentaries by Boethius, had for centuries been accepted as one of the foundations of all culture. During the lifetime of Abelard the full challenge of the Aristotelian work had not yet been presented, though it had been developing quietly along several paths, some of which were indeed rather fantastic. For instance, most of the medieval Latin translations of Aristotle stem not from the original Greek but from earlier Arabic translations.

Within the Western Christendom of the early 2nd millennium, a wholly new readiness to open the mind to the concrete reality of the world had arisen, a view of the universe and life that resembled the Aristotelian viewpoint. The tremendous eagerness with which this new philosophy was embraced was balanced, however, by a deep concern lest the continuity of tradition and the totality of truth be shattered by the violence of its assimilation. And this danger was enhanced by the fact that Aristotle's works did not come alone; they came, in fact, accompanied by the work of Arabic commentators, especially Avicenna and Averroës, and their heterodox interpretations.

The first theologian of the Middle Ages who boldly accepted the challenge of the new Aristotelianism was a 13th-century Dominican, Albertus Magnus, an encyclopedic scholar. Although he knew no Greek, he conceived a plan of making accessible to the Latin West the complete works of Aristotle, by way of commentaries and paraphrases; and, unlike Boethius, he did carry out this resolve. He also penetrated and commented upon the works of Pseudo-Dionysius; he was likewise acquainted with those of the Arabs, especially Avicenna; and he knew Augustine. Nevertheless, he was in no sense primarily a man of bookish scholarship; his strongest point, in fact, was the direct observation of nature and experimentation. After having taught for some years at the University of Paris, he travelled, as a Dominican superior, through almost all of Europe. Not only was he continually asking questions of fishermen, hunters, beekeepers, and birdcatchers but he himself also bent his sight to the things of the visible world. But amidst the most palpable descriptions of bees, spiders, and apples, recorded in two voluminous books on plants and animals, Albertus formulated completely new, and even revolutionary, methodological principles: for instance, "There can be no philosophy about concrete things," or, "in such matters only experience can provide certainty."

With Albertus, the problem of the conjunction of faith and reason had suddenly become much more difficult, because reason itself had acquired a somewhat new meaning. "Reason" implied, in his view, not only the capacity for formally correct thinking, for finding adequate creatural analogies to the truths of revelation, but it implied, above all, the capacity to grasp the reality that man encounters. Henceforth, the Boethian principle of "joining faith with reason" would entail the never-ending task of bringing belief into a meaningful coordination with the incessantly multiplying stock of natural knowledge of man and the universe. Since Albertus' nature, however, was given more to conquest than to the establishment of order, the business of integrating all of these new and naturally divergent elements into a somewhat consistent intellectual structure waited for another man, his pupil Aquinas.

To epitomize the intellectual task that Aquinas set for himself, the image of Odysseus' bow, which was so difficult to bend that an almost superhuman strength was needed, is fitting. As a young student at the University of Naples, he had met in the purest possible form both extremes, which, though they seemed inevitably to be pulling away from one another, it was nevertheless his life's task to join: one of these extremes was the dynamic, voluntary poverty movement whose key word was "the Bible"; and the second phenomenon was the Aristotelian writings and outlook, which at that time could have been encountered nowhere else in so intensive a form. And "Aristotle" meant to Aquinas not so much an individual author as a specific world view—viz., the affirmation of natural reality as a whole, including the human body and the natural human powers of cognition. To be sure, the resulting *Summa theologiae* (which Aquinas himself chose to leave incomplete) was a magnificent intellectual structure; but it was never intended to be a closed system of definitive knowledge. Aquinas could no longer possess the magnificent naiveté of Boethius, who had considered it possible to discuss the Trinitarian God without resorting to the Bible, nor could he share Anselm's conviction that Christian faith so completely concurred with natural reason that it could be proved on compelling rational grounds.

In the meanwhile, the poles of the controversy—the biblical impulses, on the one hand, and the philosophical and secular ones, on the other—had begun to move vigorously apart, and partisans moving in both directions found some encouragement in Aquinas himself. But in his later years he realized that the essential compatibility as well as the relative autonomy of these polar positions and the necessity for their conjunction had to be clarified anew by going back to a deeper root of both—that is, to a more consistent understanding of the concepts of creation and createdness. At Paris, he had to defend his own idea of "a theologically based worldliness and a theology open to the world" not only against the secularistic "philosophism" of Siger of Brabant, a stormy member of the faculty of arts, and against an aggressive group of heterodox Aristotelians around him, but also (and even more) against the traditional (Augustinian) objection that by advocating the rights of all natural things Aquinas would encroach upon the rights of God, and that, besides, the theologian needs to know only that part of creation that is pertinent to his theological subject. The latter idea was supported also by the Italian mystical theologian Bonaventure, who, in his earlier days as a colleague of Aquinas at the university, had likewise been enamoured of Aristotle, but later, alarmed by the secularism that was growing in the midst of Christendom, became more mistrustful of the capacities of natural reason. Aquinas answered this objection in somewhat the following way: The benefit that the theologian may derive from an investigation of natural reality cannot be determined in advance, but, in general, faith presupposes and therefore needs natural knowledge of the world; at times, an error concerning the creation leads people astray also from the truth of faith. This may sound like an optimistic rationalism; but the corrective of negative theology and philosophy was always present in the mind of Thomas, as well. Not only, as he argued in his treatise on God, do humans not know what God is, but they do not know the essences of things either.

The remainder of this chapter will discuss in detail the lives and work of the leading Scholastic philosophers of the 12th and 13th centuries.

ALEXANDER OF HALES

(b. *c.* 1170/85, Hales, Gloucestershire, Eng.—d. 1245, Paris, France)

Alexander of Hales was a theologian and philosopher whose doctrines influenced the teachings of such thinkers as Bonaventure and John of La Rochelle. The *Summa theologica,* for centuries ascribed to him, is largely the work of followers.

Alexander studied and taught in Paris, receiving the degrees of master of arts (before 1210) and theology (1220). He was archdeacon of Coventry in 1235 and became a Franciscan (*c.*. 1236). In Paris he founded the Schola Fratrum Minorum, where he was the first holder, possibly until his death, of the Franciscan chair.

Only the most general features of Alexander's theology and philosophy have been made clear: basically an Augustinian, he had to some extent taken into account the psychological, physical, and metaphysical doctrines of Aristotle, while discarding popular Avicennian tenets of emanations from a Godhead. The "Franciscan" theories of matter and form in spiritual creatures, of the multiplicity of forms, and of illumination combined with experience are probably Alexander's adaptations of similar theories of the Augustinian and other traditions. His original works, apart from sections of the *Summa* and of an *Expositio regulae* ("Exposition of the Rule"), include a commentary on the *Four Books of Sentences* of Peter Lombard—the first to treat the *Sentences,* rather than the Bible, as the basic text in theology; *Quaestiones disputatae antequam esset frater* ("Questions Before Becoming a Brother..."); *Quodlibeta;* sermons; and a treatise on difficult words entitled *Exoticon.* Alexander was known to the Scholastics by the title Doctor Irrefragabilis (Impossible to Refute).

ROBERT GROSSETESTE

(b. *c.* 1175, Suffolk, Eng.—d. Oct. 9, 1253, Buckden, Buckinghamshire)

Robert Grosseteste was an English bishop and scholar who introduced into the world of European Christendom Latin translations of Greek and Arabic philosophical and scientific writings. His philosophical thinking—a somewhat eclectic blend of Aristotelian and Neoplatonic ideas—consistently searched for a rational scheme of things, both natural and divine.

Grosseteste was educated at the University of Oxford and then held a position with William de Vere, the bishop of Hereford. Grosseteste was chancellor of Oxford from about 1215 to 1221 and was given thereafter a number of ecclesiastical preferments and sinecures from which he resigned in 1232. From 1229 or 1230 to 1235 he was first lecturer in theology to the Franciscans, on whom his influence was profound. The works of this, his pre-episcopal career, include a commentary on Aristotle's *Posterior Analytics* and *Physics,* many independent treatises on scientific subjects, and several scriptural commentaries.

Grosseteste became bishop of Lincoln in 1235 and held this office until his death. His career as a bishop (during which he translated, among other works, Aristotle's *Nichomachean Ethics* from the Greek) was remarkable for his ruthless pursuit of three abiding principles: a belief in the supreme importance of the cure of souls, a highly centralized and hierarchical conception of the church, and a conviction of the superiority of the church over the state. His challenge of the widespread practice of endowing officials in the service of the crown and papacy with ecclesiastical benefices intended for the cure of souls brought him into conflict with both. He attended the Council of Lyon (1245) and argued before the papal curia at Lyon (1250).

Grosseteste was deeply interested in scientific method, which he described as both inductive and deductive. By the observation of individual events in nature, human beings advance to a general law, called a "universal experimental principle," which accounts for these events. Experimentation either verifies or falsifies a theory by testing its empirical consequences. For Grosseteste, the study of nature is impossible without mathematics. He cultivated the science of optics (*perspectiva*), which measures the behaviour of light by mathematical means. His studies of the rainbow and comets employ both observation and mathematics. His treatise *De luce* (1215–20; *On Light*) presents light as the basic form of all things and God as the primal, uncreated light.

Grosseteste's pupil Roger Bacon (*c.* 1220–1292) made the mathematical and experimental methods the key to natural science. The term *experimental science* was popularized in the West through his writings.

WILLIAM OF AUVERGNE

(b. after 1180, Aurillac, Aquitaine, France—d. 1249, Paris)

William of Auvergne, also known as William of Paris, was the most prominent French philosopher-theologian of the early 13th century and one of the first Western scholars to attempt to integrate Classical Greek and Arabic philosophy with Christian doctrine.

William became a master of theology at the University of Paris in 1223 and a professor by 1225. He was named bishop of the city in 1228. As such, he defended the rising mendicant orders (i.e., religious orders whose corporate as well as personal poverty made it necessary for them to beg alms) against attacks by the secular clergy, which impugned the mendicants' orthodoxy and reason for existence. As a reformer, he limited the clergy to one benefice (church office) at a time if it provided them sufficient means.

William's principal work, written between 1223 and 1240, is the monumental *Magisterium divinale* ("The Divine Teaching"), a seven-part compendium of philosophy and theology: *De primo principio,* or *De Trinitate* ("On the First Principle," or "On the Trinity"); *De universo creaturarum* ("On the Universe of Created Things"); *De anima* ("On the Soul"); *Cur Deus homo* ("Why God Became Man"); *De sacramentis* ("On the Sacraments"); *De fide et legibus* ("On Faith and Laws"); and *De virtutibus et moribus* ("On Virtues and Customs").

After the condemnation of Aristotle's *Physics* and *Metaphysics* in 1210 by church authorities fearful of their negative effect on the Christian faith, William initiated the attempt to delete those Aristotelian theses that he saw as incompatible with Christian beliefs. On the other hand, he strove to assimilate into Christianity whatever in Aristotle's thought is consistent with it.

Influenced by the Aristotelianism of Avicenna and by the Neoplatonism of Augustine and the School of Chartres, William nevertheless was sharply critical of those elements in Classical Greek philosophy that contradicted Christian theology, specifically on the questions of human freedom, Divine Providence, and the individuality of the soul. He opposed the Aristotelian doctrine of the eternity of the world as contrary to the Christian notion of creation. His critique of Avicenna emphasized the latter's conception of God and creation. Against the determinism of Avicenna, whose God creates the universe eternally and necessarily through the mediation of 10 intelligences, William defended the Christian notion of a God who creates the world freely and directly. Creatures are radically contingent and dependent on God's creative will. Unlike God, they do not exist necessarily; indeed, their existence is distinct from their essence and accidental to it. God has no essence distinct from his existence; he is pure existence. In stressing the essential instability and temporality of the world, William attributed true existence and causality to God alone. Although a follower of Augustine, William, like others of his time, was compelled to rethink the older Augustinian notions in terms of the newer Aristotelian and Avicennian philosophies.

SAINT ALBERTUS MAGNUS

(b. c. 1200, Lauingen an der Donau, Swabia [Germany] — d. Nov. 15, 1280, Cologne),

Albertus Magnus ("Albert the Great") was a Dominican bishop and philosopher best known as a teacher of Thomas Aquinas and as a proponent of Aristotelianism at the University of Paris. He established the study of nature as a legitimate science within the Christian tradition. By papal decree in 1941, he was declared the patron saint of all who cultivate the natural sciences. He was the most prolific writer of his century and was the only scholar of his age to be called "the Great"; this title was used even before his death.

Albertus was the eldest son of a wealthy German lord. After his early schooling, he went to the University of

Albertus Magnus, detail of a fresco by Tommaso da Modena, c. 1352; in the Church of San Nicolo, Treviso, Italy. Alinari/Art Resource, New York

Padua, where he studied the liberal arts. He joined the Dominican order at Padua in 1223. He continued his studies at Padua and Bologna and in Germany and then taught theology at several convents throughout Germany, lastly at Cologne.

Sometime before 1245 he was sent to the Dominican convent of Saint-Jacques at the University of Paris, where he came into contact with the works of Aristotle, newly translated from Greek and Arabic, and with the commentaries on Aristotle's works by Averroës, a 12th-century Spanish-Arabian philosopher. At Saint-Jacques he lectured on the Bible for two years and then for another two years on Peter Lombard's *Sentences,* the theological textbook of the medieval universities. In 1245 he was graduated master in the theological faculty and obtained the Dominican chair "for foreigners."

It was probably at Paris that Albertus began working on a monumental presentation of the entire body of knowledge of his time. He wrote commentaries on the Bible and on the *Sentences;* he alone among medieval scholars made commentaries on all the known works of Aristotle, both genuine and spurious, paraphrasing the originals but frequently adding "digressions" in which he expressed his own observations, "experiments," and speculations. The term *experiment* for Albertus indicates a careful process of observing, describing, and classifying. His speculations were open to Neoplatonic thought. Apparently in response to a request that he explain Aristotle's *Physics,* Albertus undertook—as he states at the beginning of his *Physica*—"to make . . . intelligible to the Latins" all the branches of natural science, logic, rhetoric, mathematics, astronomy, ethics, economics, politics, and metaphysics. While he was working on this project, which took about 20 years to complete, he probably had among his disciples Aquinas, who arrived at Paris late in 1245.

Albertus distinguished the way to knowledge by revelation and faith from the way of philosophy and of science; the latter follows the authorities of the past according to their competence, but it also makes use of observation and proceeds by means of reason and intellect to the highest degrees of abstraction. For Albertus these two ways are not opposed; there is no "double truth"—one truth for faith and a contradictory truth for reason. All that is really true is joined in harmony. Although there are mysteries accessible only to faith, other points of Christian doctrine are recognizable both by faith and by reason—e.g., the doctrine of the immortality of the individual soul. He defended this doctrine in several works against the teaching of the Averroists, who held that only one intellect, which is common to all human beings, remains after the death of the individual.

Albertus's lectures and publications gained him great renown. He came to be quoted as readily as the Arabian philosophers Avicenna and Averroës and even Aristotle himself. His contemporary, Roger Bacon—who was by no means friendly toward Albertus—spoke of him as "the most noted of Christian scholars."

In the summer of 1248, Albertus was sent to Cologne to organize the first Dominican *studium generale* ("general house of studies") in Germany. He presided over the house until 1254 and devoted himself to a full schedule of studying, teaching, and writing. During this period his chief disciple was Aquinas, who returned to Paris in 1252. The two men maintained a close relationship even though doctrinal differences began to appear. From 1254 to 1257 Albertus was provincial of "Teutonia," the German province of the Dominicans. Although burdened with added administrative duties, he continued his writing and scientific observation and research.

Albertus resigned the office of provincial in 1257 and resumed teaching in Cologne. In 1259 he was appointed by the pope to succeed the bishop of Regensburg, and he was installed as bishop in January 1260. After Alexander IV died in 1261, Albertus was able to resign his episcopal see. He then returned to his order and to teaching at Cologne. From 1263 to 1264 he was legate of Pope Urban IV, preaching the crusade throughout Germany and Bohemia; subsequently, he lectured at Würzburg and at Strasbourg. In 1270 he settled definitively at Cologne, where, as he had done in 1252 and in 1258, he made peace between the archbishop and his city.

During his final years he made two long journeys from Cologne. In 1274 he attended the second Council of Lyon, France, and spoke in favour of acknowledging Rudolf of

Habsburg as German king. In 1277 he traveled to Paris to uphold the recently condemned good name and writings of Aquinas, who had died a few years before, and to defend certain Aristotelian doctrines that both he and Aquinas held to be true.

Albertus's works represent the entire body of European knowledge of his time not only in theology but also in philosophy and the natural sciences. His importance for medieval science essentially consists in his bringing Aristotelianism to the fore against reactionary tendencies in contemporary theology. On the other hand, without feeling any discrepancy in it, he also gave the widest latitude to Neoplatonic speculation, which was continued by Ulrich of Strasbourg and by the German mystics of the 14th century. It was by his writings on the natural sciences, however, that he exercised the greatest influence. Albertus must be regarded as unique in his time for having made accessible and available the Aristotelian knowledge of nature and for having enriched it by his own observations in all branches of the natural sciences. A preeminent place in the history of science is accorded to him because of this achievement.

SAINT BONAVENTURE

(b. c. 1217, Bagnoregio, Papal States—d. July 15, 1274, Lyon [France]),

Bonaventure was a leading medieval theologian, minister general of the Franciscan order, and cardinal bishop of Albano. He wrote several works on the spiritual life and recodified the constitution of his order (1260). He was declared a doctor (teacher) of the church in 1587.

He was a son of Giovanni of Fidanza, a physician, and Maria of Ritella. He fell ill while a boy and, according to his own words, was saved from death by the intercession

of St. Francis of Assisi. Entering the University of Paris in 1235, he received the master of arts degree in 1243 and then joined the Franciscan order, which named him Bonaventure in 1244. He studied theology in the Franciscan school at Paris from 1243 to 1248. His masters, especially Alexander of Hales, recognized in him a student with a keen memory and unusual intelligence. He was also under the tutelage of John of La Rochelle. After their deaths (1245) he studied further under Eudes Rigauld and William of Meliton. He was later probably influenced by the Dominican Guerric of Saint-Quentin.

By turning the pursuit of truth into a form of divine worship, he integrated his study of theology with the Franciscan mode of the mendicant life. In 1248, he began to teach the Bible; from 1251 to 1253 he lectured on the *Sentences,* of Peter Lombard, and he became a master of theology in 1254, when he assumed control of the Franciscan school in Paris. He taught there until 1257, producing many works, notably commentaries on the Bible and the *Sentences* and the *Breviloquium* ("Summary"), which presented a summary of his theology. These works showed his deep understanding of Scripture and the early Church Fathers—principally Augustine—and a wide knowledge of the philosophers, particularly Aristotle.

Bonaventure was particularly noted in his day as a man with the rare ability to reconcile diverse traditions in theology and philosophy. Bonaventure admired Aristotle as a natural scientist, but he preferred Plato and Plotinus, and above all Augustine, as metaphysicians. His main criticism of Aristotle and his followers was that they denied the existence of divine ideas. As a result, Aristotle was ignorant of exemplarism (God's creation of the world according to ideas in his mind) and also of divine providence and government of the world. This involved Aristotle in a threefold blindness: he taught that the world is eternal, that all people share one agent intellect (the active principle of understanding), and that there are no rewards or punishments after death. Plato and Plotinus avoided these mistakes, but because they lacked Christian faith, they could not see the whole truth. For Bonaventure, faith alone enables one to avoid error in these important matters.

Bonaventure did not confuse philosophy with theology. Philosophy is knowledge of the things of nature and the soul that is innate in human beings or acquired through their own efforts, whereas theology is knowledge of heavenly things that is based on faith and divine revelation. Bonaventure, however, rejected the practical separation of philosophy from theology. Philosophy needs the guidance of faith; far from being self-sufficient, it is but a stage in a progression toward the higher knowledge that culminates in the vision of God.

For Bonaventure, every creature to some degree bears the mark of its Creator. The soul has been made in the very image of God. Thus, the universe is like a book in which the triune God is revealed. His *Itinerarium mentis in Deum* (1259; *The Soul's Journey into God*) follows Augustine's path to God, from the external world to the interior world of the mind and then beyond the mind from the temporal to the eternal. Throughout this journey, human beings are aided by a moral and intellectual divine illumination. The mind has been created with an innate idea of God so that, as Anselm pointed out, humans cannot think that God does not exist. In a terse reformulation of the Anselmian argument for God's existence, Bonaventure states that if God is God, he exists.

In 1256 Bonaventure defended the Franciscan ideal of the Christian life against William of Saint-Amour, a university teacher who accused the mendicants of defaming the Gospel by their practice of poverty and who wanted to prevent the Franciscans and their fellow mendicants, the Dominicans, from attaining teaching positions. Bonaventure's defense of the Franciscans and his personal probity as a member of his religious order led to his election as minister general of the Franciscans on Feb. 2, 1257.

Founded by St. Francis according to strict views about poverty, the Franciscan order was at that time undergoing internal discord. One group, the Spirituals, disrupted the order by a rigorous view of poverty; another, the Relaxati, disturbed it by a laxity of life. Bonaventure used his authority so prudently that, placating the first group and reproving the second, he preserved the unity of the order and reformed it in the spirit of St. Francis. The work of restoration and reconciliation owed its success to Bonaventure's tireless visits, despite delicate health, to each province of the order and to his own personal realization of the Franciscan ideal. In his travels, he preached the Gospel constantly and so elegantly that he was recognized everywhere as a most eloquent preacher. Revered by his order, Bonaventure recodified its constitutions (1260), wrote for it a new *Life of St. Francis of Assisi* (1263), and protected it (1269) from an assault by Gerard of Abbeville, a teacher of theology at Paris, who renewed the charge of William of Saint-Amour. He also protected the church during the period 1267–73 by upholding the Christian faith while denouncing the views of unorthodox masters at Paris who contradicted revelation in their philosophy.

Bonaventure's wisdom and ability to reconcile opposing views moved Pope Gregory X to name him cardinal bishop of Albano, Italy, in May 1273, though Bonaventure had declined to accept appointment to the see of York, England, from Pope Clement IV in 1265. Gregory consecrated him in November at Lyon, where he resigned as minister general of the Franciscans in May 1274. At the second Council of Lyon he was the leading figure in the reform of the church, reconciling the secular (parish) clergy with the mendicant orders. He also had a part in restoring the Greek church to union with Rome. His death, at the council, was viewed as the loss of a wise and holy man, full of compassion and virtue, captivating with love all who knew him. He was buried the same day in a Franciscan church with the pope in attendance. The respect and love that was held for Bonaventure is exemplified in the formal announcement of the council: "At the funeral there was much sorrow and tears; for the Lord has given him this grace, that all who saw him were filled with an immense love for him." His exemplary life as a Franciscan and the continual influence of his doctrine on the life and devotion of the Western church won for him a declaration of sanctity by Pope Sixtus IV; he was designated a doctor of the church by Sixtus V.

Modern scholars consider Bonaventure to have been one of the foremost intellectual and spiritual leaders of his age, an intrepid defender of human and divine truth, and an outstanding exponent of a mystical and Christian wisdom.

HENRY OF GHENT

(b. *c.* 1217, Ghent, Flanders [now in Belgium]—d. June 29, 1293, Tournai)

Henry of Ghent was a Scholastic philosopher and theologian, one of the most illustrious teachers of his time, who was a great adversary of Aquinas and whose controversial writings influenced his contemporaries and followers, particularly postmedieval Platonists.

After studying at Tournai, where he became a canon in 1267, he studied theology at Paris; there, from 1276 (when he was archdeacon of Bruges) to 1292 he became famous as a lecturer. In 1278 he was archdeacon of Tournai and was a member of the commission that drafted the famous condemnation (1277) of Averroism (after the interpretation of Aristotle by the Muslim philosopher Averroës). His violent opposition (1282–90) to the mendicant orders led to his being censured in 1290 by Cardinal Benedict Caetani, later Pope Boniface VIII. Among the several councils that he attended were those of Lyon (1274), Cologne, and Compiègne, France.

Henry was an eclectic, neither Aristotelian nor Augustinian. He taught that matter could be created by God to exist independent of form. He denied a real distinction between essence and existence and between the soul and its faculties. A voluntarist, he regarded reason as being related to will as servant to master and declared that conscience is entirely in the will, being a choice of the will that never disagrees with right reason.

Henry has been generally neglected by historians because of the inaccessibility of his works. Significant for the development of ethical theory in the European Middle Ages, however, is the fact that the great Scottish philosopher John Duns Scotus devoted much of his energy to answering Henry's arguments. Despite attacks from other eminent thinkers, such as William of Ockham and Durandus of Saint-Pourçain, Henry's writings were widely read between the 14th and 18th century. During the 16th century the Servites erroneously adopted him as their official doctor.

ROGER BACON

(b. *c.* 1220, Ilchester, Somerset, or Bisley, Gloucester?, Eng.—d. 1292, Oxford?)

Roger Bacon was an English Franciscan philosopher and educational reformer who was a major medieval proponent of experimental science. Bacon studied mathematics, astronomy, optics, alchemy, and languages. He was the first European to describe in detail the process of making gunpowder, and he proposed flying machines and motorized ships and carriages. Bacon (as he himself complacently remarked) displayed a prodigious energy and zeal in the pursuit of experimental science; indeed, his studies were talked about everywhere and eventually won him a place in popular literature as a kind of wonder worker. Bacon therefore represents a historically precocious expression of the empirical spirit of experimental science, even though his actual practice of it seems to have been exaggerated.

Roger Bacon. Hulton Archive/Getty Images

EARLY LIFE

Bacon was born into a wealthy family; he was well-versed in the classics and enjoyed the advantages of an early training in geometry, arithmetic, music, and astronomy. Inasmuch as he later lectured at Paris, it is probable that his master of arts degree was conferred there, presumably not before 1241—a date in keeping with his claim that he saw Alexander of Hales (who died in 1245) with his own eyes and that he heard William of Auvergne dispute twice in the presence of the whole university.

UNIVERSITY AND SCIENTIFIC CAREER

In the earlier part of his career, Bacon lectured in the faculty of arts on Aristotelian and pseudo-Aristotelian treatises, displaying no indication of his later preoccupation with science. His Paris lectures, important in enabling scholars to form some idea of the work done by one who was a pioneer in introducing the works of Aristotle into western Europe, reveal an Aristotelianism strongly marked by Neoplatonist elements stemming from many different sources. The influence of Avicenna on Bacon has been exaggerated.

About 1247 a considerable change took place in Bacon's intellectual development. From that date forward he expended much time and energy and huge sums of money in experimental research, in acquiring "secret" books, in the construction of instruments and of tables, in the training of assistants, and in seeking the friendship of savants—activities that marked a definite departure from the usual routine of the faculty of arts. The change was probably caused by his return to Oxford and the influence there of Robert Grosseteste and his student Adam de Marisco, as well as that of Thomas Wallensis, the bishop of St. David's. From 1247 to 1257, Bacon devoted himself wholeheartedly to the cultivation of those new branches of learning to which he was introduced at Oxford—languages, optics, and alchemy—and to further studies in astronomy and mathematics. It is true that Bacon was more skeptical of hearsay claims than were his contemporaries, that he suspected rational deductions (holding to the superior dependability of confirming experiences), and that he extolled experimentation so ardently that he has often been viewed as a harbinger of modern science more than 300 years before it came to bloom. Yet, research on Bacon suggests that his characterization as an experimenter may be overwrought. His originality lay not so much in any positive contribution to the sum of knowledge as in his insistence on fruitful lines of research and methods of experimental study. For him, human beings acquire knowledge through reasoning and experience, but without the latter there can be no certitude. Humans gain experience through the senses and also through an interior divine illumination that culminates in mystical experience. Bacon was critical of the methods of Parisian theologians such as Albertus Magnus and Aquinas. He strove to create a universal wisdom embracing all the sciences and organized by theology.

As for actual experiments performed, he deferred to a certain Master Peter de Maricourt (Maharn-Curia), a Picard, who alone, he wrote, understood the method of experiment and whom he called *dominus experimentorum* ("master of experiments"). Bacon, to be sure, did have a sort of laboratory for alchemical experiments and carried out some systematic observations with lenses and mirrors. His studies on the nature of light and on the rainbow are especially noteworthy, and he seems to have planned and interpreted these experiments carefully. But his most notable "experiments" seem never to have been actually performed; they were merely described. He suggested, for example, that a balloon of thin copper sheet be made and filled with "liquid fire"; he felt that it would float in the air as many light objects do in water. He seriously studied the problem of flying in a machine with flapping wings. He was the first person in the West to give exact directions for making gunpowder (1242); and, though he knew that if confined, it would have great power and might be useful in war, he failed to speculate further. (Its use in guns arose early in the following century.) Bacon described spectacles (which also soon came into use); elucidated the principles of reflection, refraction, and spherical aberration; and proposed mechanically propelled ships and carriages. He used a camera obscura (which projects an image through a pinhole) to observe eclipses of the Sun.

CAREER AS A FRIAR

In 1257 another marked change took place in Bacon's life. Because of ill health and his entry into the Order of Friars Minor, Bacon felt (as he wrote) forgotten by everyone and all but buried. His university and literary careers seemed finished. His feverish activity, his amazing credulity, his superstition, and his vocal contempt for those not sharing his interests displeased his superiors in the order and brought him under severe discipline. He decided to appeal to Pope Clement IV, whom he may have known when the latter was (before his election to the papacy) in the service of the Capetian kings of France. In a letter (1266) the pope referred to letters received from Bacon, who had come forward with certain proposals covering the natural world, mathematics, languages, perspective, and astrology. Bacon had argued that a more accurate experimental knowledge of nature would be of great value in confirming the Christian faith, and he felt that his proposals would be of great importance for the welfare of the church and of the universities. The pope desired to become more fully informed of these projects and commanded Bacon to send him the work. But Bacon had had in mind a vast encyclopaedia of all the known sciences, requiring many collaborators, the organization and administration of which would be coordinated by a papal institute. The work, then, was merely projected when the pope thought that it already existed. In obedience to the pope's command, however, Bacon set to work and in a remarkably short time had dispatched the *Opus majus* ("Great Work"), the *Opus minus* ("Lesser Work"), and the *Opus tertium* ("Third Work"). He had to do this secretly and notwithstanding any command of his superiors to the contrary; and even when the irregularity of his conduct attracted their attention and the terrible weapons of spiritual coercion were brought to bear upon him, he was deterred from explaining his position by the papal command of secrecy. Under the circumstances, his achievement was truly astounding. He reminded the pope that, like the leaders of the schools with their commentaries and scholarly summaries, he could have covered quires of vellum with "puerilities" and vain speculations. Instead, he aspired to penetrate realms undreamed of in the schools at Paris and to lay bare the secrets of nature by positive study. The *Opus majus* was an effort to persuade the pope of the urgent necessity and manifold utility of the reforms that he proposed. But the death of Clement in 1268 extinguished Bacon's dreams of gaining for the sciences their rightful place in the curriculum of university studies.

Bacon projected yet another encyclopaedia, of which only fragments were ever published, namely, the *Communia naturalium* ("General Principles of Natural Philosophy") and the *Communia mathematica* ("General Principles of Mathematical Science"), written about 1268. In 1272 there appeared the *Compendium philosophiae* ("Compendium of Philosophy"). In philosophy—and even Bacon's so-called scientific works contain lengthy philosophical digressions—he was the disciple of Aristotle; even though he did incorporate Neoplatonist elements into his philosophy, his thought remains essentially Aristotelian in its main lines.

Sometime between 1277 and 1279, Bacon was condemned to prison by his fellow Franciscans because of certain "suspected novelties" in his teaching. The condemnation was probably issued because of his bitter attacks on the theologians and scholars of his day, his excessive credulity in alchemy and astrology, and his penchant for millenarianism under the influence of the prophecies of Joachim of Fiore. How long he was imprisoned is unknown. His last work (1292), incomplete as so many others, shows him as aggressive as ever.

SAINT THOMAS AQUINAS

(b. 1224/25, Roccasecca, near Aquino, Terra di Lavoro, Kingdom of Sicily—d. March 7, 1274, Fossanova, near Terracina, Latium, Papal States)

Thomas Aquinas was an Italian Dominican theologian, the foremost medieval Scholastic. He developed his own conclusions from Aristotelian premises, notably in the metaphysics of personality, creation, and Providence. As a theologian he was responsible in his two masterpieces, the *Summa theologiae* and the *Summa contra gentiles,* for the classical systematization of Latin theology; and as a poet he wrote some of the most gravely beautiful eucharistic hymns in the church's liturgy. His doctrinal system and the explanations and developments made by his followers are known as Thomism. Although many modern Roman Catholic theologians do not find St. Thomas altogether congenial, he is nevertheless recognized by the Roman Catholic Church as its foremost Western philosopher and theologian.

EARLY YEARS

Thomas was born to parents who were in possession of a modest feudal domain on a boundary constantly disputed by the emperor and the pope. His father was of Lombard origin; his mother was of the later invading Norman strain. His people were distinguished in the service of Emperor Frederick II during the civil strife in southern Italy between the papal and imperial forces. Thomas was placed in the monastery of Monte Cassino near his home as an oblate (i.e., offered as a prospective monk) when he was still a young boy; his family doubtless hoped that he would someday become abbot to their advantage. In 1239, after nine years in this sanctuary of spiritual and cultural life, young Thomas was forced to return to his family when the emperor expelled the monks because they were too obedient to the pope. He was then sent to the University of Naples, recently founded by the emperor, where he first encountered the scientific and philosophical works that were being translated from the Greek and the Arabic. In this setting Thomas decided to join the Friars Preachers, or Dominicans, a new religious order founded 30 years earlier, which departed from the traditional paternalistic form of government for monks to the more democratic form of the mendicant friars, and from the monastic life of prayer and manual labour to a more active life of preaching and teaching. By this move he took a liberating step beyond the feudal world into which he was born and the monastic spirituality in which he was reared. A dramatic episode marked the full significance of his decision. His parents had him abducted on the road to Paris, where his shrewd superiors had immediately assigned him so that he would be out of the reach of his family but also so that he could pursue his studies in the most prestigious and turbulent university of the time.

STUDIES IN PARIS

Thomas held out stubbornly against his family despite a year of captivity. He was finally liberated and in the autumn of 1245 went to Paris to the convent of Saint-Jacques, the great university centre of the Dominicans; there he studied under Albertus Magnus.

Escape from the feudal world, rapid commitment to the University of Paris, and religious vocation to one of the new mendicant orders all meant a great deal in a world in which faith in the traditional institutional and conceptual structure was being attacked. The encounter between the gospel and the culture of his time formed the nerve centre of Thomas's position and directed its development. Normally, his work is presented as the integration into Christian thought of the recently discovered Aristotelian philosophy, in competition with the integration of Platonic thought effected by the Church Fathers during the first 12 centuries of the Common Era. This view is essentially correct; more radically, however, it should also be asserted that Aquinas's work accomplished an evangelical awakening to the need for a cultural and spiritual renewal not only in the lives of individual men but also throughout the church. Aquinas must be understood in his context as a mendicant religious, influenced both by the evangelism of St. Francis of Assisi, founder of the Franciscan order, and by the devotion to scholarship of St. Dominic, founder of the Dominican order.

When Aquinas arrived at the University of Paris, the influx of Arabian-Aristotelian science was arousing a sharp reaction among believers; and several times the church authorities tried to block the naturalism and rationalism that were emanating from this philosophy and, according to many ecclesiastics, seducing the younger generations. Thomas did not fear these new ideas, but, like his master Albertus Magnus (and Roger Bacon, also lecturing at Paris), he studied the works of Aristotle and eventually lectured publicly on them.

For the first time in history, Christian believers and theologians were confronted with the rigorous demands of scientific rationalism. At the same time, technical progress was requiring people to move from the rudimentary economy of an agrarian society to an urban society with production organized in trade guilds, with a market economy, and with a profound feeling of community. New generations of men and women, including clerics, were reacting against the traditional notion of contempt for the world and were striving for mastery over the forces of nature through the use of their reason. The structure of Aristotle's philosophy emphasized the primacy of the intelligence. Technology itself became a means of access to truth; mechanical arts were powers for humanizing the cosmos. Thus, the dispute over the reality of universals, which had dominated early Scholastic philosophy, was left behind; and a coherent metaphysics of knowledge and of the world was being developed.

During the summer of 1248, Aquinas left Paris with Albertus, who was to assume direction of the new faculty established by the Dominicans at the convent in Cologne. He remained there until 1252, when he returned to Paris to prepare for the degree of master of theology. After taking his bachelor's degree, he received the *licentia docendi* ("license to teach") at the beginning of 1256 and shortly afterward finished the training necessary for the title and privileges of master. Thus, in the year 1256 he began teaching theology in one of the two Dominican schools incorporated in the University of Paris.

YEARS AT THE PAPAL CURIA AND RETURN TO PARIS

In 1259 Thomas was appointed theological adviser and lecturer to the papal Curia, then the centre of Western humanism. He returned to Italy, where he spent two years at Anagni at the end of the reign of Alexander IV and four years at Orvieto with Urban IV. From 1265 to 1267 he taught at the convent of Santa Sabina in Rome and then, at the request of Clement IV, went to the papal Curia in Viterbo. Suddenly, in November 1268, he was sent to Paris, where he became involved in a sharp doctrinal polemic that had just been triggered off.

The works of Averroës, who was known as the great commentator and interpreter of Aristotle, were just becoming known to the Parisian masters. There seems to be no doubt about the Islamic faith of the Cordovan philosopher; nevertheless, he asserted that the structure of religious knowledge was entirely heterogeneous to rational knowledge: two truths—one of faith, the other of reason—can, in the final analysis, be contradictory. This dualism was denied by Muslim orthodoxy and was still less acceptable to Christians. With the appearance of Siger of Brabant, however, and from 1266 on, the quality of Averroës's exegesis and the wholly rational bent of his thought began to attract disciples in the faculty of arts at the University of Paris. Aquinas rose in protest against his colleagues; nevertheless, the parties retained a mutual esteem. As soon as he returned from Italy, he began to dispute with Siger, who, he claimed, was compromising not only orthodoxy but also the Christian interpretation of Aristotle. Aquinas found himself wedged in between the Augustinian tradition of thought, now more emphatic than ever in its criticism of Aristotle, and the Averroists. Radical Averroism was condemned in 1270, but at the same time Aquinas, who sanctioned the autonomy of reason under faith, was discredited.

In the course of this dispute, the very method of theology was called into question. According to Aquinas, reason is able to operate within faith and yet according to its own laws. The mystery of God is expressed and incarnate in human language; it is thus able to become the object of an active, conscious, and organized elaboration in which the rules and structures of rational activity are integrated in the light of faith. In the Aristotelian sense of the word, then (although not in the modern sense), theology is a "science"; it is knowledge that is rationally derived from propositions that are accepted as certain because they are revealed by God. The theologian accepts authority and faith as his starting point and then proceeds to conclusions using reason; the philosopher, on the other hand, relies solely on the natural light of reason. Aquinas was the first to view theology expressly in this way or at least to present it systematically, and in doing so he raised a storm of opposition in various quarters. Even today this opposition endures, especially among religious enthusiasts for whom reason remains an intruder in the realm of mystical communion, contemplation, and the sudden ecstasy of evangelical fervour.

The literary form of Aquinas's works must be appreciated in the context of his methodology. He organized his teaching in the form of "questions," in which critical research is presented by pro and con arguments, according to the pedagogical system then in use in the universities. Forms varied from simple commentaries on official texts to written accounts of the public disputations, which were significant events in medieval university life. Thomas's works are divided into three categories: (1) commentaries on such works as the Old and New Testaments, the *Sentences* of Peter Lombard (the official manual of theology in the universities), and the writings of Aristotle; (2) disputed questions, accounts of his teaching as a master in the disputations; (3) two *summae* or personal syntheses, the *Summa contra gentiles* and the *Summa theologiae*, which were presented as integral introductions for the use of beginners. Numerous *opuscula* ("little works"), which have great interest because of the particular circumstances that provoked them, must also be noted.

The logic of Aquinas's position regarding faith and reason required that the fundamental consistency of the realities of nature be recognized. A *physis* ("nature") has necessary laws; recognition of this fact permits the construction of a science according to a *logos* ("rational structure"). Aquinas thus avoided the temptation to sacralize the forces of nature through a naïve recourse to the miraculous or the Providence of God. For him, a whole "supernatural" world that cast its shadow over things and human beings, in Romanesque art as in social customs, had blurred people's imaginations. Nature, discovered in its profane reality, should assume its proper religious value and lead to God by more rational ways, yet not simply as a shadow of the supernatural. This understanding is exemplified in the way that Francis of Assisi admired the birds, the plants, and the Sun.

The inclusion of Aristotle's *Physics* in university programs was not, therefore, just a matter of academic curiosity. Naturalism, however, as opposed to a sacral vision of the world, was penetrating all realms: spirituality, social customs, and political conduct. About 1270, Jean de Meun, a French poet of the new cities and Thomas's neighbour in the Rue Saint-Jacques in Paris, gave expression in his *Roman de la Rose* to the coarsest realism, not only in examining the physical universe but also in describing and judging the laws of procreation. Innumerable manuscripts of the Roman poet Ovid's *Ars amatoria* (*Art of Love*) were in circulation; André le Chapelain, in his *De Deo amoris* (*On the God of Love*) adapted a more refined version for the public. Courtly love in its more seductive forms became a more prevalent element in the culture of the 13th century.

At the same time, Roman law was undergoing a revival at the University of Bologna; this involved a rigorous analysis of the natural law and provided the jurists of Frederick II with a weapon against ecclesiastical theocracy. The traditional presentations of the role and duties of princes, in which biblical symbolism was used to outline beautiful pious images, were replaced by treatises that described experimental and rational attempts at government. Aquinas had composed such a treatise—*De regimine principum* (*On the Government of Princes*)—for the king of Cyprus in 1266. In the administration of justice, juridical investigations and procedures replaced fanatical recourse to ordeals and to judgments of God.

In the face of this movement, there was a fear on the part of many that the authentic values of nature would not be properly distinguished from the disorderly inclinations of mind and heart. Theologians of a traditional bent firmly resisted any form of a determinist philosophy which, they believed, would atrophy liberty, dissolve personal responsibility, destroy faith in Providence, and deny the notion of a gratuitous act of creation. Imbued with Augustine's doctrines, they asserted the necessity and power of grace for a nature torn asunder by sin. The optimism of the new theology concerning the religious value of nature scandalized them.

Although he was an Aristotelian, Aquinas was certain that he could defend himself against a heterodox interpretation of "the Philosopher," as Aristotle was known. Aquinas held that human liberty could be defended as a rational thesis while admitting that determinations are found in nature. In his theology of Providence, he taught a continuous creation, in which the dependence of the created on the creative wisdom guarantees the reality of the order of nature. God moves sovereignly all that he creates; but the supreme government that he exercises over the universe is conformed to the laws of a creative Providence that wills each being to act according to its proper nature. This autonomy finds its highest realization in the rational creature: humans are literally self-moving

St. Thomas Aquinas. Hulton Archive/Getty Images

in their intellectual, volitional, and physical existence. Human freedom, far from being destroyed by the relationship between humans and God, finds its foundation in this very relationship. "To take something away from the perfection of the creature is to abstract from the perfection of the creative power itself." This metaphysical axiom, which is also a mystical principle, is the key to Aquinas's spirituality.

LAST YEARS AT NAPLES

At Easter time in 1272, Aquinas returned to Italy to establish a Dominican house of studies at the University of Naples. This move was undoubtedly made in answer to a request made by King Charles of Anjou, who was anxious to revive the university. After participating in a general chapter, or meeting, of the Dominicans held in Florence during Pentecost week and having settled some family affairs, Aquinas resumed his university teaching at Naples in October and continued it until the end of the following year.

Although Aquinas's argument with the Averroists had for years been matched by a controversy with the Christian masters who followed the traditional Augustinian conception of humanity as fallen, this latter dispute now became more pronounced. In a series of university conferences in 1273, Bonaventure, who was a friendly colleague of Aquinas at Paris, renewed his criticism of the Aristotelian current of thought, including the teachings of Aquinas. He criticized the thesis that philosophy is distinct from theology, as well as the notion of a physical nature that has determined laws; he was especially critical of the theory that the soul is bound up with the body as the two necessary principles that make up the nature of man and also reacted strongly to the

Aristotelians' denial of the Platonic-Augustinian theory of knowledge based upon exemplary Ideas or Forms.

The disagreement was profound. Certainly, all Christian philosophers taught the distinction between matter and spirit. This distinction, however, could be intelligently held only if the internal relationship between matter and spirit in individual human beings was sought. It was in the process of this explanation that differences of opinion arose—not only intellectual differences between idealist and realist philosophers but also emotional differences. Some viewed the material world merely as a physical and biological reality, a stage on which the history of spiritual persons is acted out, their culture developed, and their salvation or damnation determined. This stage itself remains detached from the spiritual event, and the history of nature is only by chance the setting for the spiritual history. The history of nature follows its own path imperturbably; in this history, humans are foreigners, playing a brief role only to escape as quickly as possible from the world into the realm of pure spirit, the realm of God.

Aquinas, on the contrary, noted the inclusion of the history of nature in the history of the spirit and at the same time noted the importance of the history of spirit for the history of nature. Humanity is situated ontologically (i.e., by its very existence) at the juncture of two universes, "like a horizon of the corporeal and of the spiritual." In humanity there is not only a distinction between spirit and nature but there is also an intrinsic homogeneity of the two. Aristotle furnished Aquinas with the categories necessary for the expression of this concept: the soul is the "form" of the body. For Aristotle, form is that which makes a thing to be what it is; form and matter—that out of which a thing is made—are the two intrinsic causes that constitute every material thing. For Aquinas, then, the body is the matter and the soul is the form of humans. The objection was raised that he was not sufficiently safeguarding the transcendence of the spirit, the doctrine that the soul survives after the death of the body.

Aquinas never compromised Christian doctrine by bringing it into line with the current Aristotelianism; rather, he modified and corrected the latter whenever it clashed with Christian belief. The harmony he established between Aristotelianism and Christianity was not forced but achieved by a new understanding of philosophical principles, especially the notion of being, which he conceived as the act of existing (*esse*). For him, God is pure being. Creatures participate in being according to their essence; for example, human beings participate in being, or the act of existing, to the extent that their humanity, or essence, permits. The fundamental distinction between God and creatures is that creatures have a real composition of essence and existence, whereas God's essence is his existence.

In January 1274 Aquinas was personally summoned by Gregory X to the second Council of Lyons, which was an attempt to repair the schism between the Latin and Greek churches. On his way he was stricken by illness; he stopped at the Cistercian abbey of Fossanova, where he died on March 7. In 1277 the masters of Paris, the highest theological jurisdiction in the church, condemned a series of 219 propositions; 12 of these propositions were theses of Aquinas. This was the most serious condemnation possible in the Middle Ages; its repercussions were felt in the development of ideas. It produced for several centuries a certain unhealthy spiritualism that resisted the cosmic and anthropological realism of Aquinas.

Assessment

The biography of Aquinas is one of extreme simplicity; it chronicles little but some modest travel during a career devoted entirely to university life: at Paris, the Roman Curia, Paris again, and Naples. It would be a mistake, however, to judge that his life was merely the quiet life of a professional teacher untouched by the social and political affairs of his day. The drama that went on in his mind and in his religious life found its causes and produced its effects in the university. In the young universities all the ingredients of a rapidly developing civilization were massed together, and to these universities the Christian church had deliberately and authoritatively committed its doctrine and its spirit. In this environment, Aquinas found the technical conditions for elaborating his work—not only the polemic occasions for turning it out but also the enveloping and penetrating spiritual milieu needed for it. It is within the homogeneous contexts supplied by this environment that it is possible today to discover the historical intelligibility of his work, just as they supplied the climate for its fruitfulness at the time of its birth.

Aquinas was canonized a saint in 1323, officially named doctor of the church in 1567, and proclaimed the protagonist of orthodoxy during the modernist crisis at the end of the 19th century. This continuous commendation, however, cannot obliterate the historical difficulties in which he was embroiled in the 13th century during a radical theological renewal—a renewal that was contested at the time and yet was brought about by the social, cultural, and religious evolution of the West. Aquinas was at the heart of the doctrinal crisis that confronted Christendom when the discovery of Greek science, culture, and thought seemed about to crush it. William of Tocco, Aquinas's first biographer, who had known him and was able to give evidence of the impression produced by his master's teaching, says:

> *Brother Thomas raised new problems in his teaching, invented a new method, used new systems of proof. To hear him teach a*

new doctrine, with new arguments, one could not doubt that God, by the irradiation of this new light and by the novelty of this inspiration, gave him the power to teach, by the spoken and written word, new opinions and new knowledge.

SIGER OF BRABANT

(b. *c.* 1240, duchy of Brabant—d. between 1281 and 1284, Orvieto, Tuscany)

Siger of Brabant was a professor of philosophy at the University of Paris and the leader of a school of radical, or heterodox, Aristotelianism, which arose in Paris when Latin translations of Greek and Arabic works in philosophy introduced new material to masters in the faculty of arts.

Beginning about 1260 Siger and some of his colleagues inaugurated purely rational lectures that reinterpreted works of Aristotle without regard for established teachings of the church, which had blended orthodox Aristotelianism with Christian faith. Because Averroës was the recognized commentator on Aristotle, Siger and his followers generally interpreted Aristotle's thought in an Averroistic way. Hence, in their own day they were known as "Averroists"; today they are often called "Latin Averroists" because they taught in Latin. In addition to Aristotle and Averroës, Siger's sources included such philosophers as Proclus (410–485), Avicenna, and Aquinas.

From 1266, when his name first appears, to 1276, Siger was prominent in the disputes at Paris over Aristotelianism. Bonaventure, the minister general of the Order of Friars Minor, and Aquinas, head of the Dominicans, both attacked Siger's teachings. In 1270 the bishop of Paris, Étienne Tempier, condemned 13 errors in the teaching of Siger and his partisans. Six years later the inquisitor of the Roman Catholic Church in France summoned Siger and two others suspected of heterodoxy, but they fled to Italy, where they probably entered an appeal before the papal tribunal. After Tempier announced the condemnation of 219 more propositions in 1277, Siger is believed to have been restricted to the company of a cleric, for he was stabbed at Orvieto by his cleric, who had gone mad, and he died during Martin IV's pontificate, sometime before Nov. 10, 1284. Dante, in the *Divine Comedy,* put Siger in the Heaven of Light in the brilliant company of 12 illustrious souls.

Siger's written works gradually came to light, and 14 authentic works and 6 probably authentic commentaries on Aristotle were known by the mid-20th century. Among them are *Quaestiones in metaphysicam, Impossibilia* (six exercises in sophistry) and *Tractatus de anima intellectiva* ("Treatise on the Intellectual Soul"). The last discusses his basic belief that there is only one "intellectual" soul for humankind and thus one will. Although this soul is eternal, individual human beings are not immortal. This view, though not lucidly expressed, suggests Siger's disregard for doctrines of the church and his emphasis on maintaining the autonomy of philosophy as a self-sufficient discipline.

GILES OF ROME

(b. *c.* 1243–47, Rome [Italy]—d. 1316, Avignon, France)

Giles of Rome was a Scholastic theologian, philosopher, logician, archbishop, and general and intellectual leader of the Order of the Hermit Friars of St. Augustine.

Giles joined the Augustinian Hermits in about 1257 and in 1260 went to Paris, where he was educated in the house of his order. While in Paris from 1269 to 1272, he probably studied under Aquinas, whose philosophical doctrines he defended against the ecclesiastical condemnation of 1277. Giles sided with theologians of a traditionalist cast against the Latin Averroists, whose rationalism was perceived as a threat to the Christian faith. Giles's *Errores philosophorum* (1270; *The Errors of the Philosophers*), was an attack on Averroist philosophies. His *Theoremata de esse et essentia* ("Essays on Being and Essence"), which supported the Thomistic doctrine of substance, raised a storm of opposition from other theologians, forcing Giles to take refuge in Bayeux, France (1278–80).

In 1281 he returned to Italy and was made provincial of his order in 1283 and vicar-general in 1285. That year Pope Honorius IV effected Giles' reinstatement at the University of Paris, where he taught theology until 1291. He served as general of the Augustinian Hermits from 1292 to 1295, when Pope Boniface VIII made him archbishop of Bourges, France. During the political conflict between Boniface and King Philip IV the Fair of France, Giles wrote, in 1301, a defense of the pope, *De ecclesiastica potestate* ("On the Church Power"); he proposed that the pope must have direct political power over the whole of humankind.

Developing in an original way the doctrines of Augustine and Aquinas, Giles's vast literary production includes Aristotelian and biblical commentaries and theological and political treatises. Numerous editions of his collected and individual works appeared in the 15th, 16th, and 17th centuries. His commentaries on Aristotle's entire *Organon* (i.e., the logical writings) are considered valuable by logicians.

CHAPTER 5

THE LATE MEDIEVAL PERIOD

The condemnation of 219 propositions by the masters of Paris (1277), questionable though it may have been in its methods and personal motivations, was not only understandable; it was unavoidable, since it was directed against what, after all, amounted in principle to an antitheological, rationalistic secularism. Quite another matter, however, were the practical effects of the edict, which were rather disastrous. Above all, two of the effects were pernicious: instead of free disputes among individuals, organized blocks (or "schools") now began to form; and the cooperative dialogue between theology and philosophy turned into mutual indifference or distrust.

In the Dominican order, Thomism, the theological and philosophical system of Thomas Aquinas, was made the official teaching, though the Dominicans did not always adhere to it rigorously. Averroism, cultivated by philosophers such as John of Jandun (c. 1286–1328), remained a significant, though sterile, movement into the Renaissance. In the Franciscan order, John Duns Scotus (c. 1266–1308) and William of Ockham (c. 1285–c. 1347) developed new styles of theology and philosophy that vied with Thomism throughout the late Middle Ages.

OVERVIEW OF LATE MEDIEVAL PHILOSOPHY

Near the end of the Middle Ages, some of the most creative minds were turning away from Aristotelianism and looking to newer ways of thought. Some late Scholastic philosophers were increasingly dissatisfied with Aristotle's mechanistic conception of the universe, which they found uncongenial to Christian doctrines regarding the omnipotence and absolute freedom of God. They also criticized the rationalists' insistence on the validity of the truths of reason as against the truths of faith. Although the philosophy of Aristotle, in its various interpretations, continued to be taught in the universities, by the 14th century it had lost much of its vitality and creativity. Indeed, Christian philosophers were once again finding inspiration in Neoplatonism, and the Platonism of the Renaissance would be directly continuous with the Platonism of the late Middle Ages.

The trend away from Aristotelianism was accentuated by the German Dominican Meister Eckhart (*c.* 1260–*c.* 1327), who developed a speculative mysticism of both Christian and Neoplatonic inspiration. Eckhart depicted the ascent of the soul to God in Neoplatonic terms: by gradually purifying itself from the body, the soul transcends being and knowledge until it is absorbed in the One. The soul is then united with God at its highest point, or "citadel." God himself transcends being and knowledge. Sometimes Eckhart describes God as the being of all things. This language, which was also used by Erigena and other Christian Neoplatonists, leaves him open to the charge of pantheism; but for Eckhart there is an infinite gulf between creatures and God. Eckhart meant that creatures have no existence of their own but are given existence by God, as the body is made to exist and is contained by the soul. Eckhart's profound influence can be seen in the flowering of mysticism in the German Rhineland in the late Middle Ages.

Duns Scotus opposed the rationalists' contention that philosophy is self-sufficient and adequate to satisfy the human desire for knowledge. In fact, he claimed that a pure philosopher, such as Aristotle, could not truly understand the human condition because he was ignorant of the Fall of Man and his need for grace and redemption. Unenlightened by Christian revelation, Aristotle mistook humankind's present fallen state, in which all knowledge comes through the senses, for its natural condition, in which the object of knowledge would be coextensive with all being, including the being of God. The limitation of Aristotle's philosophy was apparent to Duns Scotus in the Aristotelian proof of the existence of God as the primary mover of the universe. More adequate than this physical proof, he contended, is his own very intricate metaphysical demonstration of the existence of God as the absolutely primary, unique, and infinite being. He incorporated the Anselmian argument into this demonstration. For Duns Scotus, the notion of infinite being, not that of primary mover or being itself, is humankind's most perfect concept of God.

In opposition to the Greco-Arabic view of the government of the universe from above by necessary causes, Duns Scotus stressed the contingency of the universe and its total dependence on God's infinite creative will. He adopted the traditional Franciscan voluntarism, elevating the will above the intellect in human beings.

Duns Scotus's doctrine of universals justly earned him the title "Doctor Subtilis." Universals, in his view, exist only as abstract concepts, but they are based on common natures, such as humanity, which exist, or can exist, in many individuals. Common natures are real, and they have a real unity of their own distinct from the unity of the individuals in which they exist. The individuality of each individual is due to an added positive reality that makes the common nature a specific individual—e.g., Socrates. Duns Scotus calls such a reality an "individual difference," or "thisness" (*haecceitas*). It is an original development of the earlier medieval realism of universals.

In the late 14th century, Thomism and Scotism were called the "old way" (*via antiqua*) of philosophizing, in contrast to the "modern way" (*via moderna*) begun by philosophers such as William of Ockham. Ockham, no less than Duns Scotus, wanted to defend the Christian doctrine of the freedom and omnipotence of God and the contingency of creatures against the necessitarianism of Greco-Arabic philosophy. But for him the freedom of God is incompatible with the existence of divine ideas as positive models of creation. God does not use preconceived ideas when he creates, as Duns Scotus maintained, but he fashions the universe as he wishes. As a result, creatures have no natures, or essences, in common. There are no realities but individual things, and these have nothing in common. They are more or less like each other, however, and on this basis human beings can form universal concepts of them and talk about them in general terms.

The absolute freedom of God was often used by Ockham as a principle of philosophical and theological explanation. Because the order of nature has been freely created by God, it could have been different: fire, for example, could cool as it now heats. If God wishes, he can give us the sight, or "intuitive knowledge," of a star without the reality of the star. The moral order could also have been different. God could have made hating him meritorious instead of loving him. It was typical of Ockham not to put too much trust in the power of human reason to reach the truth. For him, philosophy must often be content with probable arguments, as in establishing the existence of the Christian God. Faith alone gives certitude in this and in other vital matters. Another principle invoked by Ockham is that a plurality is not to be posited without necessity. This principle of economy of thought, later stated as "beings are not to be multiplied without necessity," is called "Ockham's razor."

Ockhamism was censured by a papal commission at Avignon in 1326, and in 1474 it was forbidden to be taught at Paris. Nevertheless, it spread widely in the late Middle Ages and rivaled Thomism and Scotism in popularity. Other Scholastics in the 14th century shared Ockham's basic principles and contributed with him to skepticism and probabilism in philosophy. John of Mirecourt (flourished 14th century) stressed the absolute power of God and the divine will to the point of making God the cause of human sin. Nicholas of Autrecourt (c. 1300–c. 1350) adopted a skeptical attitude regarding matters such as the ability of human beings to prove the existence of God and the reality of substance and causality. Rejecting Aristotelianism as inimical to the Christian faith, he advocated a return to the atomism of the ancient Greeks as a more adequate explanation of the universe.

Nicholas of Cusa (1401–64) also preferred the Neoplatonists to the Aristotelians. To him the philosophy of Aristotle is an obstacle to the mind in its ascent to God because its primary rule is the principle of contradiction, which denies the compatibility of contradictories. But God is the "coincidence of opposites." Because he is infinite, he embraces all things in perfect unity; he is at once the maximum and the minimum. Nicholas uses mathematical symbols to illustrate how, in infinity, contradictories coincide. If a circle is enlarged, the curve of its circumference becomes less; if a circle is infinite, its circumference is a straight line. As for human knowledge of the infinite

Detail of the Pope's palace in Avignon, France. © www.istockphoto.com/
Daniel Leppens

God, one must be content with conjecture or approxima-
tion to the truth. The absolute truth escapes human
beings; their proper attitude is "learned ignorance."

For Nicholas, God alone is absolutely infinite. The universe reflects this divine perfection and is relatively infinite.
It has no circumference, for it is limited by nothing outside
of itself. Neither has it a centre; the Earth is neither at the
centre of the universe nor is it completely at rest. Place and
motion are not absolute but relative to the observer. This
new, non-Aristotelian conception of the universe anticipated some of the features of modern theories.

The remainder of this chapter will discuss in detail the
lives and work of the major philosophers of the late
Middle Ages.

MEISTER ECKHART

(b. *c.* 1260, Hochheim?, Thuringia [now in Germany]—d. 1327/28?, Avignon, France)

Meister Eckhart ("Master Eckhart") was the greatest German speculative mystic. In the transcripts of his sermons in German and Latin, he charts the course of union between the individual soul and God.

Johannes Eckhart entered the Dominican order when he was 15 and studied in Cologne, perhaps under the Scholastic philosopher Albert the Great. The intellectual background there was influenced by the great Dominican theologian Thomas Aquinas, who had recently died. In his mid-30s, Eckhart was nominated vicar (the main Dominican official) of Thuringia. Before and after this assignment he taught theology at Saint-Jacques's priory in Paris. It was also in Paris that he received a master's degree (1302) and consequently was known as Meister Eckhart.

Eckhart wrote four works in German that are usually called "treatises." At about the age of 40 he wrote the *Talks of Instruction,* on self-denial, the nobility of will and intellect, and obedience to God. In the same period, he faced the Franciscans in some famous disputations on theological issues. In 1303 he became provincial (leader) of the Dominicans in Saxony, and three years later vicar of Bohemia. His main activity, especially from 1314, was preaching to the contemplative nuns established throughout the Rhine River valley. He resided in Strasbourg as a prior.

The best-attested German work of this middle part of his life is the *Book of Divine Consolation,* dedicated to the Queen of Hungary. The other two treatises were *The Nobleman* and *On Detachment.* The teachings of the mature Eckhart describe four stages of the union between the soul and God: dissimilarity, similarity, identity, break-through. At the outset, God is all, the creature is nothing; at the ultimate stage, "the soul is above God." The driving power of this process is detachment.

1. **Dissimilarity:** "All creatures are pure noth-ingness. I do not say they are small or petty: they are pure nothingness." Whereas God inherently possesses being, creatures do not possess being but receive it derivatively. Outside God, there is pure nothingness. "The being (of things) is God." The "noble man" moves among things in detachment, knowing that they are nothing in themselves and yet aware that they are full of God—their being.

2. **Similarity:** The person thus detached from the singular (individual things) and attached to the universal (Being) discovers himself to be an image of God. Divine resemblance, an assimi-lation, then emerges: the Son, image of the Father, engenders himself within the detached soul. As an image, "thou must be in Him and for Him, and not in thee and for thee."

3. **Identity:** Eckhart's numerous statements on identity between God and the soul can be eas-ily misunderstood. He never has substantial identity in mind, but God's operation and man's becoming are considered as one. God is no longer outside man, but he is perfectly inte-riorized. Hence such statements: "The being and the nature of God are mine; Jesus enters the castle of the soul; the spark in the soul is beyond time and space; the soul's light is uncre-ated and cannot be created, it takes possession

of God with no mediation; the core of the soul and the core of God are one."

4. **Breakthrough:** To Meister Eckhart, identity with God is still not enough; to abandon all things without abandoning God is still not abandoning anything. The human individual must live "without why." He must seek nothing, not even God. Such a thought leads man into the desert, anterior to God. For Meister Eckhart, God exists as "God" only when the creature invokes him. Eckhart calls "Godhead" the origin of all things that is beyond God (God conceived as Creator). "God and the Godhead are as distinct as heaven and earth." The soul is no longer the Son. The soul is now the Father: it engenders God as a divine person. "If I were not, God would not be God." Detachment thus reaches its conclusion in the breakthrough beyond God. If properly understood, this idea is genuinely Christian: it retraces, for the believer, the way of the Cross of Christ.

These teachings are to be found in his Latin works too. But the Latin *Sermons, Commentaries on the Bible* and *Fragments* are more Scholastic and do not reveal the originality of his thought. Nevertheless, Eckhart enjoyed much respect even among scholars. In his 60th year he was called to a professorship at Cologne. Heinrich von Virneburg—a Franciscan, unfavourable to Dominicans, anyway—was the archbishop there, and it was before his court that the now immensely popular Meister Eckhart was first formally charged with heresy. To a list of errors, he replied by publishing a Latin *Defense* and then asked to be transferred to the pope's court in Avignon. When ordered to justify a new series of propositions drawn from his writings, he declared: "I may err but I am not a heretic, for the first has to do with the mind and the second with the will!" Before judges who had no comparable mystical experience of their own, Eckhart referred to his inner certainty: "What I have taught is the naked truth." The bull of Pope John XXII, dated March 27, 1329, condemns 28 propositions extracted from the two lists. Since it speaks of Meister Eckhart as already dead, it is inferred that Eckhart died some time before, perhaps in 1327 or 1328. It also says that Eckhart had retracted the errors as charged.

Although Eckhart's philosophy amalgamates Greek, Neoplatonic, Arabic, and Scholastic elements, it is unique. His doctrine, sometimes abstruse, always arises from one simple, personal mystical experience to which he gives a number of names. By doing so, he was also an innovator of the German language, contributing many abstract terms.

JOHN DUNS SCOTUS

(b. c. 1266, Duns, Lothian [now in Scottish Borders], Scot.—d. Nov. 8, 1308, Cologne [Germany])

John Duns Scotus was first and foremost an influential realist philosopher and scholastic theologian. He also pioneered the classical defense of the doctrine that Mary, the mother of Jesus, was conceived without original sin (the Immaculate Conception), and he argued that the Incarnation was not dependent on the fact that man had sinned, that will is superior to intellect and love to knowledge, and that the essence of heaven consists in beatific love rather than the vision of God.

John Duns Scotus. Hulton Archive/Getty Images

EARLY LIFE AND CAREER

There is perhaps no other great medieval thinker whose life is as little known as that of Duns Scotus. Yet, patient research in recent times has unearthed a number of facts. Early 14th-century manuscripts, for instance, state explicitly that John Duns was a Scot, from Duns, who belonged to the English province of Friars Minor (the order founded by Francis of Assisi), that "he flourished at Cambridge, Oxford, and Paris and died in Cologne."

Although accounts of his early schooling and entry into the Franciscan Order are unreliable, Duns Scotus would have learned as a novice of St. Francis's personal love for Christ in the Eucharist, his reverence for the priesthood, and his loyalty to "the Lord Pope"—themes given special emphasis in Duns Scotus's own theology. In addition, he would have studied interpretations of St. Francis's thought, particularly those of Bonaventure, who saw the Franciscan ideal as a striving for God through learning that will culminate in a mystical union of love. In his early *Lectura Oxoniensis,* Duns Scotus insisted that theology is not a speculative but a practical science of God and that humanity's ultimate goal is union with the divine Trinity through love. Although this union is known only by divine revelation, philosophy can prove the existence of an infinite being, and herein lies its merit and service to theology. Duns Scotus's own intellectual journey to God is to be found in his prayerful *Tractatus de primo principio* (*A Treatise on God As First Principle*), perhaps his last work.

Jurisdictionally, the Scots belonged to the Franciscan province of England, whose principal house of studies was at the University of Oxford, where Duns Scotus apparently spent 13 years (1288–1301) preparing for inception as master of theology. There is no record of where he took the eight years of preliminary philosophical training (four for a bachelor's and four for the master's degrees) required to enter such a program.

After studying theology for almost four years, John Duns was ordained priest by Oliver Sutton, bishop of Lincoln (the diocese to which Oxford belonged). Records show the event took place at St. Andrew's Church in Northampton on March 17, 1291. In view of the minimum age requirements for the priesthood, this suggests that

Duns Scotus must have been born no later than March 1266, certainly not in 1274 or 1275 as earlier historians maintained.

Duns Scotus would have spent the last four years of the 13-year program as bachelor of theology, devoting the first year to preparing lectures on Peter Lombard's *Four Books of Sentences* and the second to delivering them. A bachelor's role at this stage was not to give a literal explanation of this work but rather to pose and solve questions of his own on topics that paralleled subject "distinctions" in Lombard. Consequently, the questions Duns Scotus discussed in his *Lectura Oxoniensis* ranged over the whole field of theology. When he had finished, he began to revise and enlarge them with a view to publication. Such a revised version was called an *ordinatio,* in contrast to his original notes (*lectura*) or a student report (*reportatio*) of the actual lecture. If such a report was corrected by the lecturer himself, it became a *reportatio examinata.* From a date mentioned in the prologue, it is clear that in 1300 Duns Scotus was already at work on his monumental Oxford commentary on the *Sentences,* known as the *Ordinatio* or *Opus Oxoniense.*

Statutes of the university required that the third year be devoted to lectures on the Bible; and, in the final year, the bachelor *formatus,* as he was called, had to take part in public disputations under different masters, including his own. In Duns Scotus's case, this last year can be dated rather precisely, for his name occurs among the 22 Oxford Franciscans, including the two masters of theology, Adam of Howden and Philip of Bridlington, who were presented to Bishop Dalderby on July 26, 1300, for faculties, or the proper permissions to hear confessions of the great crowds that thronged to the Franciscans' church in the city. Because the friars had but one chair of theology and the list of trained bachelors waiting to incept was long, regent masters were replaced annually. Adam was the 28th and Philip the 29th Oxford master, so that Philip's year of regency was just beginning. It must have coincided with Duns Scotus's final and 13th year because an extant disputation of Bridlington as master indicates John Duns was the bachelor respondent. This means that by June of 1301 he had completed all the requirements for the mastership in theology; yet, in view of the long line ahead of him, there was little hope of incepting as master at Oxford for perhaps a decade to come.

YEARS AT THE UNIVERSITY OF PARIS

When the turn came for the English province to provide a talented candidate for the Franciscan chair of theology at the more prestigious University of Paris, Duns Scotus was appointed. One *reportatio* of his Paris lectures indicates that he began commenting on the *Sentences* there in the autumn of 1302 and continued to June 1303. Before the term ended, however, the university was affected by the long-smouldering feud between King Philip IV and Pope Boniface VIII. The issue was taxation of church property to support the king's wars with England. When Boniface excommunicated him, the monarch retaliated by calling for a general church council to depose the pope. He won over the French clergy and the university. On June 24, 1303, a great antipapal demonstration took place. Friars paraded in the Paris streets. Berthold of Saint-Denis, bishop of Orleans and former chancellor of the university, together with two Dominicans and two Franciscans, addressed the meeting. On the following day royal commissioners examined each member of the Franciscan house to determine whether he was with or against the king. Some 70 friars, mostly French, sided with Philip, while the rest (some 80 odd) remained loyal to the pope, among them John Duns

This medieval illustration shows a class at the University of Paris.
Fotosearch/Hulton Archive/Getty Images

Scotus and Master Gonsalvus Hispanus. The penalty was exile from France within three days. Boniface countered with a bull of August 15 suspending the university's right to give degrees in theology or canon and civil law. As a result of his harassment and imprisonment by the king's minister, however, Boniface died in October and was succeeded by Pope Benedict XI. In the interests of peace, Benedict lifted the ban against the university in April 1304, and shortly afterwards the king facilitated the return of students.

Where Duns Scotus spent the exile is unclear. Possibly his Cambridge lectures stem from this period, although they may have been given during the academic year of 1301–02 before coming to Paris. At any rate, Duns Scotus was back before the summer of 1304, for he was the bachelor respondent in the *disputatio in aula* ("public disputation") when his predecessor, Giles of Ligny, was promoted to master. On November 18 of that same year, Gonsalvus, who had been elected minister general of the Franciscan order at the Pentecost chapter, or meeting, assigned as Giles's successor "Friar John Scotus, of whose laudable life, excellent knowledge, and most subtle ability as well as his other remarkable qualities I am fully informed, partly from long experience, partly from report which has spread everywhere."

The period following Duns Scotus's inception as master in 1305 was one of great literary activity. Aided by a staff of associates and secretaries, he set to work to complete his *Ordinatio* begun at Oxford, using not only the Oxford and Cambridge lectures but also those of Paris. A search of manuscripts reveals a magisterial dispute Duns Scotus conducted with the Dominican master, Guillaume Pierre Godin, against the thesis that matter is the principle of individuation (the metaphysical principle that makes an individual thing different from other things of the same species), but so far no questions publicly disputed *ordinarie*—i.e., in regular turn with the other regent masters—have been discovered. There is strong evidence, however, that some questions of this sort existed but were eventually incorporated into the *Ordinatio*. Duns Scotus did conduct one solemn quodlibetal disputation, so called because the master accepted questions on any topic (*de quodlibet*) and from any bachelor or master present (*a quodlibet*). The 21 questions Duns Scotus treated were later revised, enlarged, and organized under two main topics, God and creatures. Although less extensive in scope than the *Ordinatio,* these *Quaestiones quodlibetales* are scarcely less important because they represent his most mature thinking. Indeed, Duns Scotus's renown depends principally on these two major works.

The short but important *Tractatus de primo principio,* a compendium of what reason can prove about God, draws heavily upon the *Ordinatio.* The remaining authentic works seem to represent questions discussed privately for the benefit of the Franciscan student philosophers or theologians. They include, in addition to the *Collationes* (from both Oxford and Paris), the *Quaestiones in Metaphysicam Aristotelis* and a series of logical questions occasioned by the Neoplatonist Porphyry's *Isagoge* and Aristotle's *De praedicamentis,*

De interpretatione, and *De sophisticis elenchis.* These works certainly postdate the Oxford *Lectura* and may even belong to the Parisian period. Antonius Andreus, an early follower who studied under Duns Scotus at Paris, expressly says his own commentaries on Porphyry and *De praedicamentis* are culled from statements of Duns Scotus *sedentis super cathedram magistralem* ("sitting on the master's chair").

FINAL PERIOD AT COLOGNE

In 1307 Duns Scotus was appointed professor at Cologne. Some have suggested that Gonsalvus sent Scotus to Cologne for his own safety. His controversial claim that Mary need never have contracted original sin seemed to conflict with the doctrine of Christ's universal redemption. Duns Scotus's effort was to show that the perfect mediation would be preventative, not merely curative. Although his brilliant defense of the Immaculate Conception marked the turning point in the history of the doctrine, it was immediately challenged by secular and Dominican colleagues. When the question arose in a solemn quodlibetal disputation, the secular master Jean de Pouilly, for example, declared the Scotist thesis not only improbable but even heretical. Should anyone be so presumptuous as to assert it, he argued impassionedly, one should proceed against him "not with arguments but otherwise." At a time when Philip IV had initiated heresy trials against the wealthy Knights Templars, Pouilly's words have an ominous ring. There seems to have been something hasty about Duns Scotus's departure in any case. Writing a century later, the Scotist William of Vaurouillon referred to the traditional account that Duns Scotus received the minister general's letter while walking with his students and set out at once for Cologne, taking little or nothing with him. Duns Scotus lectured at Cologne until his death. His body at present lies in the nave of the Franciscan church near the Cologne cathedral, and in many places he is venerated as blessed.

Whatever the reason for his abrupt departure from Paris, Duns Scotus certainly left his *Ordinatio* and *Quodlibet*

Cologne Cathedral, surrounded by the modern city of Cologne (Koln) Germany. Vladimir Rys/Getty Images

unfinished. Eager pupils completed the works, substituting materials from *reportationes examinatae* for the questions Duns Scotus left undictated. The critical Vatican edition begun in 1950 is aimed at, among other things, reconstructing the *Ordinatio* as Duns Scotus left it, with all his corrigenda, or corrections.

Despite their imperfect form, Duns Scotus's works were widely circulated. His claim that universal concepts are based on a "common nature" in individuals was one of the central issues in the 14th-century controversy between realists and nominalists concerning the question of whether general types are figments of the mind or are real. Later, this same Scotist principle deeply influenced Charles Sanders Peirce (1839–1914), an American philosopher, who considered Duns Scotus the greatest speculative mind of the Middle Ages as well as one of the "profoundest metaphysicians that ever lived." His strong defense of the papacy against the divine right of kings made Duns Scotus unpopular with the English Reformers of the 16th century, for whom "dunce" (a Dunsman) became a word of obloquy, yet his theory of intuitive cognition suggested to John Calvin (1509–64), the Genevan Reformer, how God may be "experienced." During the 16th to 18th centuries among Catholic theologians, Duns Scotus's following rivaled that of Aquinas and in the 17th century outnumbered that of all the other schools combined.

WILLIAM OF OCKHAM

(b. *c.* 1285, Ockham, Surrey?, Eng.—d. 1347/49, Munich, Bavaria [now in Germany])

William of Ockham, a philosopher, theologian, and political writer, is regarded as the founder of a form of nominalism—the school of thought that denies that universal concepts such as "father" have any reality apart from the individual things signified by the universal or general term.

EARLY LIFE

Little is known of Ockham's childhood. It seems that he was still a youngster when he entered the Franciscan order. At that time a central issue of concern in the order and a main topic of debate in the church was the interpretation of the rule of life composed by St. Francis of Assisi concerning the strictness of the poverty that should be practiced within the order. Ockham's early schooling in a Franciscan convent concentrated on the study of logic; throughout his career, his interest in logic never waned, because he regarded the science of terms as fundamental and indispensable for practicing all the sciences of things, including God, the world, and ecclesiastical or civil institutions; in all his disputes logic was destined to serve as his chief weapon against adversaries.

After his early training, Ockham took the traditional course of theological studies at the University of Oxford and apparently between 1317 and 1319 lectured on the *Sentences* of Peter Lombard. His lectures were also set down in written commentaries, of which the commentary on Book I of the *Sentences* (his *Ordinatio*) was actually written by Ockham himself. His opinions aroused strong opposition from members of the theological faculty of Oxford, however, and he left the university without obtaining his master's degree in theology. Ockham thus remained, academically speaking, an undergraduate— known as an *inceptor* ("beginner") in Oxonian language or, to use a Parisian equivalent, a *baccalaureus formatus*.

Ockham continued his academic career, apparently in English convents, simultaneously studying points of logic in natural philosophy and participating in theological debates. When he left his country for Avignon in the autumn of 1324 at the pope's request, he was acquainted with a university environment shaken not only by disputes but also by the challenging of authority: that of the bishops in doctrinal matters and that of the chancellor of the university, John Lutterell, who was dismissed from his post in 1322 at the demand of the teaching staff.

However abstract and impersonal the style of Ockham's writings may be, they reveal at least two aspects of Ockham's intellectual and spiritual attitude: he was a theologian-logician (*theologicus logicus* is Luther's term). On the one hand, with his passion for logic he insisted on evaluations that are severely rational, on distinctions between the necessary and the incidental and differentiation between evidence and degrees of probability—an insistence that places great trust in reason and human nature. On the other hand, as a theologian he referred to the primary importance of the God of the creed whose omnipotence determines the gratuitous salvation of men; God's saving action consists of giving without any obligation and is already profusely demonstrated in the creation of nature. As noted above, the medieval rule of economy, that "beings are not to be multiplied without necessity," commonly known as Ockham's razor, was used by Ockham to eliminate many entities that had been devised, especially by the Scholastic philosophers, to explain reality.

Treatise to John XXII

Ockham met John Lutterell again at Avignon; in a treatise addressed to Pope John XXII, the former chancellor of Oxford denounced Ockham's teaching on the *Sentences*, extracting from it 56 propositions that he showed to be in serious error. Lutterell then became a member of a committee of six theologians that produced two successive reports based on extracts from Ockham's commentary, of which the second was more severely critical. Ockham, however, presented to the pope another copy of the *Ordinatio* in which he had made some corrections. It appeared that he would be condemned for his teaching, but the condemnation never came.

At the convent where he resided in Avignon, Ockham met Bonagratia of Bergamo, a doctor of civil and canon law who was being persecuted for his opposition to John XXII on the problem of Franciscan poverty. On Dec. 1, 1327, the Franciscan general Michael of Cesena arrived in Avignon and stayed at the same convent; he, too, had been summoned by the pope in connection with the dispute over the holding of property. They were at odds over the theoretical problem of whether Christ and his Apostles had owned the goods they used; that is, whether they had renounced all ownership (both private and corporate), the right of property and the right to the use of property. Michael maintained that because Christ and his Apostles had renounced all ownership and all rights to property, the Franciscans were justified in attempting to do the same thing.

The relations between John and Michael grew steadily worse, to such an extent that, on May 26, 1328, Michael fled from Avignon accompanied by Bonagratia and William. Ockham, who was already a witness in an appeal secretly drafted by Michael on April 13, publicly endorsed the appeal in September at Pisa, where the three Franciscans were staying under the protection of Emperor Louis IV the Bavarian, who had been excommunicated in 1324 and proclaimed by John XXII to have forfeited all rights to the empire. They followed him to Munich in 1330, and thereafter Ockham wrote fervently against the papacy in defense of both the strict Franciscan notion of poverty and the empire.

Instructed by his superior general in 1328 to study three papal bulls on poverty, Ockham found that they contained many errors that showed John XXII to be a heretic who had forfeited his mandate by reason of his heresy. His status of pseudo-pope was confirmed in Ockham's view in 1330–31 by his sermons proposing that the souls of the saved did not enjoy the vision of God immediately after death but only after they were rejoined with the body at the Last Judgment, an opinion that contradicted tradition and was ultimately rejected.

Nevertheless, his principal dispute remained the question of poverty, which he believed was so important for religious perfection that it required the discipline of a theory: whoever chooses to live under the evangelical rule of St. Francis follows in the footsteps of Christ who is God and therefore king of the universe but who appeared as a poor man, renouncing the right of ownership, submitting to the temporal power, and desiring to reign on this earth only through the faith vested in him. This reign expresses itself in the form of a church that is organized but has no infallible authority—either on the part of a pope or a council—and is essentially a community of the faithful that has lasted over the centuries and is sure to last for more, even though temporarily reduced to a few, or even to one; everyone, regardless of status or sex, has to defend in the church the faith that is common to all.

For Ockham the power of the pope is limited by the freedom of Christians that is established by the gospel and the natural law. It is therefore legitimate and in keeping with the gospel to side with the empire against the papacy or to defend, as Ockham did in 1339, the right of the king of England to tax church property. From 1330 to

1338, in the heat of this dispute, Ockham wrote 15 or 16 more or less political works; some of them were written in collaboration, but *Opus nonaginta dierum* ("Work of 90 Days"), the most voluminous, was written alone.

EXCOMMUNICATION

Excommunicated after his flight from Avignon, Ockham maintained the same basic position after the death of John XXII in 1334, during the reign of Benedict XII (1334–42), and after the election of Clement VI. In these final years he found time to write two treatises on logic, which bear witness to the leading role that he consistently assigned to that discipline, and he discussed the submission procedures proposed to him by Pope Clement. Ockham was long thought to have died at a convent in Munich in 1349 during the Black Death, but he may actually have died there in 1347.

JULIAN OF NORWICH

(b. 1342, probably Norwich, Norfolk, Eng.—d. after 1416)

Julian of Norwich was a celebrated mystic whose *Revelations of Divine Love* (or *Showings*) is generally considered one of the most remarkable documents of medieval religious experience. She spent the latter part of her life as a recluse at St. Julian's Church, Norwich.

On May 13, 1373, Julian was healed of a serious illness after experiencing a series of visions of Christ's suffering and of the Blessed Virgin, about which she wrote two accounts; the second, longer version was composed 20 or 30 years after the first. Unparalleled in English religious literature, *Revelations* spans the most profound mysteries of the Christian faith—such as the problems

This statue of Julian of Norwich, which appears on the west front of Norwich Cathedral, was carved by sculptor David Holgate in hard white ancaster stone in 2001. Courtesy of David Holgate with permission of Norwich Cathedral

of predestination, the foreknowledge of God, and the existence of evil. The clarity and depth of her perception, the precision and accuracy of her theological presentation, and the sincerity and beauty of her expression reveal a mind and personality of exceptional strength and charm. Never beatified, Julian is honoured on the unofficial feast day of May 13. A modern chapel in the Church of St. Julian has been dedicated to her memory.

NICHOLAS OF CUSA

(b. 1401, Kues, Trier—d. Aug. 11, 1464, Todi, Papal States)

Nicholas of Cusa was a cardinal, mathematician, scholar, experimental scientist, and influential philosopher who stressed the incomplete nature of human knowledge of God and of the universe.

At the Council of Basel in 1432, he gained recognition for his opposition to the candidate put forward by Pope Eugenius IV for the archbishopric of Trier. To his colleagues at the council he dedicated *De concordantia catholica* (1433; "On Catholic Concordance"), in which he expressed support for the supremacy of the general councils of the church over the authority of the papacy. In the same work he discussed the harmony of the church, drawing a pattern for priestly concord from his knowledge of the order of the heavens. By 1437, however, finding the council unsuccessful in preserving church unity and enacting needed reforms, Nicholas reversed his position and became one of Eugenius' most ardent followers. Ordained a priest about 1440, Cusa was made a cardinal in Brixen (Bressanone), Italy, by Pope Nicholas V and in 1450 was elevated to bishop there. For two years Cusa served as Nicholas' legate to Germany, after which he began to serve full-time as bishop of Brixen.

A model of the "Renaissance man" because of his disciplined and varied learning, Cusa was skilled in theology, mathematics, philosophy, science, and the arts. In *De docta ignorantia* (1440; "On Learned Ignorance") he described the learned man as one who is aware of his own ignorance. In this and other works he typically borrowed symbols from geometry to demonstrate his points, as in his comparison of man's search for truth to the task of converting a square into a circle.

Among Cusa's other interests were diagnostic medicine and applied science. He emphasized knowledge through experimentation and anticipated the work of the astronomer Copernicus by discerning a movement in the universe that did not centre in the Earth, although the Earth contributed to that movement. Cusa's study of plant growth, from which he concluded that plants absorb nourishment from the air, was the first modern formal experiment in biology and the first proof that air has weight. Numerous other developments, including a map of Europe, can also be traced to Cusa. A manuscript collector who recovered a dozen lost comedies by the Roman writer Plautus, he left an extensive library that remains a centre of scholarly activity in the hospital he founded and completed at his birthplace in 1458.

CONCLUSION

Not all of medieval philosophy is specifically medieval and therefore definitively belonging to the dead past; there are perennial elements that are meant for every age, the present one included, three of which may be here distinguished. First, not only has medieval philosophy held true to the normal historical rule that ideas, once thought and expressed, remain present and significant in the following time; but the medieval intellectual accomplishments have surpassed the rule and exerted, though more or less anonymously, a quite exceptional influence even on philosophers who consciously revolted against medieval philosophy in general or Scholasticism in particular. New historical investigations clearly show that the classical modern philosophers René Descartes, John Locke, Benedict de Spinoza, and G. W. Leibniz owe much to medieval ideas. Of Descartes, for instance, it has been said, contrary to the usual view, that he could quite well have been "included with the later Scholastics"; and even the American philosopher Charles Sanders Peirce, as noted earlier, held some Scholastic philosophers in very high regard. Secondly, there have been explicit attempts to go back to specifically Scholastic thinkers and inspire a renaissance of their basic ideas. Two chief movements of this kind were the Scholasticism of the Renaissance (called *Barockscholastik*) and the Neoscholasticism of the 19th and 20th centuries, both of which were primarily interested in the work of Aquinas.

Renaissance Scholasticism received its first impulses from the Reformation. One of its leading figures, a Dominican, Cardinal Thomas de Vio (16th century), commonly known as Cajetan, had some famous disputations with the great Reformer Martin Luther. Cajetan's great commentary on Aquinas, published again in a late edition of the *Summa theologiae* (1888–1906), exerted for at least three centuries an enormous influence on the formation of Catholic theology. He was much more than a commentator, however; his original treatise on the "Analogy of Names," for example, can even pass as a prelude to 20th century linguistic philosophy. The so-called Silver Age of Scholastic thought, which occurred in the 16th century, is represented by two Spaniards: Francisco de Vitoria of the first half and Francisco Suárez of the last half of the century were both deeply engaged in what has been called the "Counter-Reformation." Although likewise commentators on the works of Aquinas, the Renaissance Scholastics were much less concerned with looking back to the past than with the problems of their own epoch, such as those of international law, colonialism, resistance to an unjust government, and world community. Although Suárez was for more than a hundred years among the most esteemed authors, even in Protestant universities, Renaissance Scholasticism was eradicated by Enlightenment philosophy and German Idealism. This, in turn, gave rise in due time to the Neoscholasticism of the 19th century, one of the most effective promoters of which was a German Jesuit, Joseph Kleutgen. He published a voluminous scholarly apology of patristic and Scholastic theology and philosophy and was also responsible for the outline of the papal encyclical *Aeterni Patris* of Leo XIII (1879), which explicitly proclaimed the "instauration of Christian philosophy according to St. Thomas." The result, fed of course from many different sources, was that all over the world new centres of Scholastic research and higher learning (universities) arose—some more traditionalistic, some from the start engaged in the dialogue with modern philosophy and science, and some primarily devoted to historical studies and the preparation of critical editions of the great medieval Scholastics — and that a multitude of periodicals and systematic textbooks were produced.

It is too early for a competent judgment on this enterprise to be made. Its immeasurable educational benefit for several generations of students, however, is as undeniable as the unique contributions of some Neoscholastic thinkers to current intellectual life. A weak point, on the other hand, seems to be a somewhat "unhistorical" approach to reality and existence. In any case, it is scarcely a matter of mere chance that, after World War II, the impact of existentialism and Marxism caused a noticeable decline in Neoscholasticism and that the positions of "Scholastic" authors from the 1970s to the present have progressed well beyond Neoscholasticism.

The third and most important aspect of the enduring significance of medieval philosophy implies the acceptance of the following fundamental tenets: that there exist truths that humans know, and also revealed truths of faith; that these two kinds of truth are not simply reducible to one another; that faith and theology do not, by means of symbols and sensuous images, merely say the same as what reason and science say more clearly by conceptual argumentation (Averroës, Hegel); that, on the other hand, reason is not a "prostitute" (Luther), but is human individual's natural capacity to grasp the real world; that since reality and truth, though essentially inexhaustible, are basically one, faith and reason cannot ultimately contradict one another. Those who hold these convictions appear quite unable to refrain from trying to coordinate what they know with what they believe. Any epoch that addresses itself to this interminable task can ill afford to ignore the demanding and multiform paradigms of medieval philosophy; but to the problems posed it will have to find its own answer.

GLOSSARY

anathema Something that is intensely disliked or loathed or cursed by clerical authority.

archiepiscopal About or referring to an archbishop.

canticle Religious song or chant, taken from the Bible.

Christendom The medieval idea of Europe as one large Christian church-state, or the geographical area in which Christianity prevails.

Determinist Philosophy The belief that current events and actions are necessitated by natural laws and events that came before.

empirical Coming from experience or observation.

encomiast One who praises.

eremetical Hermitlike.

etymology The study of the history of words.

Eucharist The Christian sacrament of Communion, in which blessed wine and bread are consumed by parishioners as a ritual commemoration of Jesus's last supper.

exegesis A critical explanation of a text.

falfsifah Arabic word for philosophy.

heterodox Unconventional, contrary to traditional beliefs.

mendicant A monk or other member of a monastic religious order, such as the Franciscans, which originally relied on begging and did not own property.

metaphysics The philosophical study whose object is to determine the real nature of things—to determine the meaning, structure, and principles of whatever is insofar as it is.

oblate One who is offered as a prospective monk.

oligarchy A government controlled by a small group, especially the wealthy.

ontologically Related to the study of being in general, or of what applies neutrally to everything that is real.

Peripatetic A student at Aristotle's school the Lyceum or one who believes in the philosophical ideas of Aristotle.

polemic Fierce attack on another's beliefs or opinions.

probity Adherence to high moral principles or ideals.

psaltery An early musical instrument.

Rationalist Adherent of the philosophical view that regards reason as the chief test of knowledge.

sacralize To treat something as if it is holy.

savant An extremely learned person, especially one with knowledge in a specific field, such as mathematics or theology.

Scotism The philosophical and religious system of John Duns Scotus.

Scholasticism An elaborately structured style of philosophy that dominated medieval universities until the early 15th century.

syllogism In logic, a valid deductive argument having two premises and a conclusion, as in this example: "All men are mortal; no gods are mortal; therefore no men are gods."

Thomistic Pertaining to the doctrines and philosophy of St. Thomas Aquinas.

universals Attributes or properties shared by particular things, e.g., redness, and thought to have an independent existence.

vellum A fine-grained animal skin, such as calf, kid, or lambskin, on which texts can be written.

viz Namely, that is to say.

BIBLIOGRAPHY

HISTORIES

Étienne Gilson, *History of Christian Philosophy in the Middle Ages* (1955, reissued 1980), is the best account of medieval philosophy. Aemé Forest, Fernand van Steenberghen, and Maurice de Gandillac, *Le Mouvement doctrinal du IXe au XIVe siècle* (1951, reissued 1956), traces doctrinal developments from the 9th to the 14th century. The interpretation of 13th-century philosophy in Fernand van Steenberghen, *La Philosophie au XIIIe siècle*, 2nd ed. (1988), is different from that of Gilson; the author's *Aristotle in the West*, 2nd ed. (1970), is a valuable account of the introduction of Aristotle's works into western Europe. David Knowles, *The Evolution of Medieval Thought* (1962, reissued 1964), is the work of an eminent historian of medieval religion. Armand A. Maurer, *Medieval Philosophy*, 2nd ed. (1982), sketches medieval philosophy from Augustine to the Renaissance. Norman Kretzmann, Anthony Kenny, and Jan Pinborg (eds.), *The Cambridge History of Later Medieval Philosophy* (1982, reissued 1997), covers the period from the rediscovery of Aristotle to the decline of Scholasticism (1100–1600). The following are short accounts of philosophy in the Middle Ages: John Marenbon, *Early Medieval Philosophy (480–1150): An Introduction* (1983, reissued 1988); Gordon Leff, *Medieval Thought: St. Augustine to Ockham* (1958, reprinted 1983); Paul Vignaux, *Philosophy in the Middle Ages*, trans. by E.C. Hall (1959, reissued 1975; originally published in French, 3rd ed., 1958); and Julius R. Weinberg, *A Short History of Medieval Philosophy* (1964, reissued 1974).

Useful information about medieval Arab and Jewish philosophy is contained in T.J. de Boer, *The History of Philosophy in Islam*, trans. by Edward R. Jones (1903, reissued 1994; originally published in German, 1901); Goffredo Quadri, *La filosofia degli arabi nel suo fiore* (1939, reissued 1997); Isaac Husik, *A History of Mediaeval Jewish Philosophy* (1916, reissued 2002); and Georges Vajda, *Introduction à la pensée juive du Moyen Âge* (1947). Also of interest is Timothy C. Potts (ed.), *Conscience in Medieval Philosophy* (1980, reissued 2002).

TEXTS

Collections of translated texts include Richard McKeon (ed. and trans.), *Selections from Medieval Philosophers*, 2 vol. (1928, reissued 1958); Harry A. Wolfson, *Philo: Foundations of Religious Philosophy in Judaism, Christianity, and Islam*, 2 vol. (1947, reprinted 1968), *Philosophy of the Church Fathers*, 3rd rev. ed. (1970 —), and *The Philosophy of the Kalam* (1976), a basic study of early Arabic thought; Herman Shapiro, *Medieval Philosophy: Selected Readings from Augustine to Buridan* (1964); Arthur Hyman and James J. Walsh (eds.), *Philosophy in the Middle Ages: The Christian, Islamic, and Jewish Traditions*, 2nd ed. (1983); and John F. Wippel and Allan B. Wolter (eds.), *Medieval Philosophy: From St. Augustine to Nicholas of Cusa* (1969).

INDEX

—